YORK HANDBOOKS

GENERAL EDITOR:
Professor A.N. Jeffares
(*University of Stirling*)

ENGLISH POETRY

Clive T. Probyn

BA PH D (NOTTINGHAM) MA (VIRGINIA)
Professor of English,
Monash University, Victoria, Australia

YORK PRESS
Immeuble Esseily, Place Riad Solh, Beirut.

LONGMAN GROUP LIMITED
Longman House,
Burnt Mill,
Harlow,
Essex.

© Librairie du Liban 1984

First published 1984
Second impression 1985
ISBN 0 582 79271 1

Produced by Longman Group (FE) Ltd.
Printed in Hong Kong

Contents

Preface

This Handbook is divided into two parts. The first part (Chapters 1–4) is essentially an attempt to answer the question 'How does poetry work?', and examines its constituent parts, proceeding from space, time, sound and meaning, to the larger questions we ask about form and context. I have not tried to minimise the more technical aspects of prosody, since these are often neglected even by serious readers of poetry, nor have I pretended that they are dull and unnecessary. The further we investigate the technical aspects of poetry, the greater is our appreciation of true artistic mastery of language and form.

The second part (Chapter 5), 'Readings of poems', applies the material in Part One to whole poems (or lengthy extracts) from a wide range of poetry in English.

In addition to the acknowledgements listed on page 2, I would like to mention two studies which I found particularly helpful: Geoffrey Leech's *A Linguistic Guide to English Poetry*, Longman, London, 1969, and the as yet unpublished Cambridge doctoral thesis of Peter L. Groves, 'Shakespeare's Prosody: A New Approach to an Old Problem' (1979).

> What does it all mean, poet? Well,
> Your brains beat into rhythm, you tell
> What we felt only; you expressed
> You hold things beautiful the best,
>   And pace them in rhyme so, side by side.
> 'Tis something, nay 'tis much: but then,
> Have you yourself what's best for men?
> Are you – poor, sick, old ere your time –
> Nearer one whit your own sublime
> Than we who never have turned a rhyme?
>
> (Robert Browning, 'The Last Ride Together')

For Zoë, Andrew, Fiona

PART 1   Chapter 1
_____

Introduction

What poetry is

In Graham Greene's novel *The Power and the Glory* (1940), the whisky
priest, worn down almost to despair by a sense of spiritual inadequacy
and hunted by the state police, discovers an old school-prize anthology
of English poetry. He reads at random:

> It was a very obscure poem, full of words which were like
> Esperanto. He thought: So this is English poetry: how odd. The little
> poetry he knew dealt mainly with agony, remorse, and hope. These
> verses ended on a philosophical note – 'For men may come and men
> may go. But I go on for ever.' The triteness and untruth of 'for ever'
> shocked him a little: a poem like this ought not to be in a child's hands.
> The vulture came picking its way across the yard, a dusty and desolate
> figure: every now and then it lifted sluggishly from the earth and
> flapped down twenty yards on. The priest read:
>
> '"Come back! Come back!" he cried in grief
> Across the stormy water,
> "And I'll forgive your Highland chief –
> My daughter, O my daughter."'
>
> That sounded to him more impressive – though hardly, perhaps, any
> more than the other, stuff for children. He felt in the foreign words the
> ring of genuine passion and repeated to himself on his hot and lonely
> perch the last lines – 'My daughter, O my daughter.' The words
> seemed to contain all that he felt himself of repentance, longing, and
> unhappy love.*

By chance, the vaguely understood words of an obscure poem in a
discarded anthology unlock the reader's deepest anguish. Five words in
a foreign language, written one hundred years before, are no longer inert
but pregnant with an intensely personal significance.

There remains a mystery in the effect of poetry even for the better-
equipped reader who deliberately sets out to encounter it in his own
language. The relationship between poet and reader is like an infinitely

---

* The poem from which Greene quotes in Part II, Chapter 4 of *The Power and the Glory* is
'Lord Ullin's Daughter', by Thomas Campbell (1777–1844), and may be found in that
most famous of all poetry anthologies, F. T. Palgrave's *Golden Treasury*, first published in
1861.

renewable contract, wherein each meets the other on the shared ground of language. If, as Philip Larkin has said, a poem is 'a verbal device that would preserve an experience indefinitely by reproducing it in whoever read the poem', the task for the reader of poetry is to minimise the loss and distortion of meaning during the process of transmission from the poet's private world to the public domain, where there are limitless possibilities for misunderstanding. Winifred Nowottny has described the special challenge of understanding poetry:

> The good analytical critic is not one who strips the layers off the onion one after another until there is nothing left inside; poetic language has the quality, paradoxical in non-poetic language, that when one layer of it is stripped off, the onion looks bigger and better than it did before.*

Concentration and intensity are two of the qualities that distinguish the poetic treatment of a subject from its treatment in prose. In the following example, from Ezra Pound (1885–1972), we are shown the process whereby a poet himself strips down the onion until he is left with the essential linguistic expression of an experience, and how all other options are abandoned:

> Three years ago in Paris I got out of a 'Metro' train at La Concorde, and saw suddenly a beautiful face, and then another and another, and then a beautiful child's face, and then another beautiful woman, and I tried all that day to find words for what this had meant to me, and I could not find any words that seemed to me worthy, or as lovely as that sudden emotion . . . .
> I wrote a thirty-line poem, and destroyed it because it was what we call work 'of second intensity.' Six months later I made a poem half that length; a year later I made the following . . . sentence:
> The apparition of these faces in the crowd:
> Petals on a wet, black bough.
> I daresay it is meaningless unless one has drifted into a certain vein of thought. In a poem of this sort one is trying to record the precise instant when a thing outward and objective transforms itself, or darts into a thing inward and subjective.'†

In such a way, the intensely personal moment (the inward and subjective) has been transformed into an impersonal and communicable image of transient beauty through language. What Pound is doing here reminds us that poetic language functions at full stretch: nothing is irrelevant in its final shape.

* Winifred Nowottny, *The Language Poets Use*, Athlone Press, London, 1962, p.19: this book remains one of the best introductions to its subject.
† Ezra Pound, *Gaudier-Brzeska: A Memoir*, John Lane, London, 1916, pp.100, 103. The poem was given the title 'In a Station of the Metro'.

Poetry uses any language at the poet's disposal, but the transformation of language into poetry requires that the poet endows it with a specially significant form and context. We might say that poetry is a system of discourse which signals its presence by shape (form) and intensity of meaning (a concentration of dictionary meanings and of other, contextual meanings). Line-length is significant in poetry but not in prose (where the printer is responsible for disposing the lines on the page, not the writer). Poetry may use rhyme-schemes, a regular metre, and so on. All of these features are means to an end and except for line-length none is unique to poetry. For example, the following extract from Walter Pater's essay on Leonardo da Vinci is richly rhythmical. A 'poetic' interpretation is signalled not only by its rhythm, however, but by a particular use of language as well:

> She is older than the rocks among which she sits; like the vampire, she has been dead many times, and learned the secrets of the grave; and has been a diver in deep seas, and keeps their fallen day about her; and trafficked for strange webs with Eastern merchants; and, as Leda, was the mother of Helen of Troy, and, as Saint Anne, the mother of Mary; and all this has been to her but as the sound of lyres and flutes, and lives only in the delicacy with which it has moulded the changing lineaments, and tinged the eyelids and the hands.*

This is not *verse*, but a poetic interpretation is signalled by a distinct semantic quality: in prose, women cannot be older than rocks, but in poetry anything is possible. The marked rhythm underpins the poetic quality of this passage and provides another signal to the reader, but it is the language use which determines that we read this passage as prose poetry. By contrast, the following passage from Dr Johnson's (1709–84) *Life of Dryden* (John Dryden, 1631–1700), whilst also highly rhythmical, contains no 'poetic' use of language:

> They [Dryden's sentences] have not the formality of a settled style, in which the first half of the sentence betrays the other. The clauses are never balanced, nor the periods modelled; every word seems to drop by chance, though it falls into its proper place. Nothing is cold or languid; the whole is airy, animated and vigorous; what is little, is gay; what is great is splendid. He may be thought to mention himself too frequently, but while he forces himself upon our esteem, we cannot refuse him to stand high in his own. Every thing is excused by the play of images and the spriteliness of expression. Though all is easy, nothing is feeble; though all seems careless, there is nothing harsh;

* 'Leonardo da Vinci' is the sixth chapter of Pater's *The Renaissance* (1873). This description of La Gioconda, or Mona Lisa, was indeed chopped up into line-lengths by W. B. Yeats and printed as the first 'poem' in the *Oxford Book of Modern Verse, 1892–1935*, Oxford, 1936.

and though, since his earlier works, more than a century has passed, they have nothing yet uncouth or obsolete.

This piece of transparently clear and judicious prose requires no help from imagery or implied meanings, yet its appeal is not entirely dependent on our rational intellects for its persuasiveness. The *rhythm* of its utterance quietly underpins the prose meaning by a pleasing sense of architectural symmetry: the shape is part of its total meaning.

Prose thus borrows from poetry, but poetry borrows from everywhere. If the following poem were to be heard only, and not read, perhaps most of its listeners would be unable to say whether it was poetry at all, since it transmits none of the more obvious formal characteristics of poetry:

I have a picture I took in Bombay
of a beggar asleep on the pavement:
grey-haired, wearing shorts and a dirty shirt,
his shadow thrown aside like a blanket.

His arms and legs could be cracks in the stone,
routes for the ants' journeys, the flies' descents.
Brain-washed by the sun into exhaustion,
he lies veined in stone, a fossil man.

Behind him there is a crowd passingly
bemused by a pavement trickster and quite
indifferent to this very common sight
of an old man asleep on the pavement.

I thought it then a good composition
and glibly called it 'The Man in the Street,'
remarking how typical it was of
India that the man in the street lived there.

His head in the posture of one weeping
into a pillow chides me now for my
presumption at attempting to compose
art out of his hunger and solitude.*

Seeing as well as hearing this poem, however, suggests that great care has been taken with its shape. It is written in syllabics (there are ten syllables in each line), and has a stanzaic form. The prose-like flatness of the opening three lines is checked in the fourth line, and the second stanza begins to weave around the subject a cruelly fanciful patter of images which exploits the beggar's misery for the sake of a good composition in words, rather like a tourist might take a photograph of quaintly picturesque squalor. It is a poem about the guilt of writing

* 'Decomposition', by Zulfikar Ghose, from *Jets from Orange*, Macmillan, London, 1967.

dishonestly, about the conscious 'application' of poetic devices in order to conceal or transform into 'art' another's misery. Here, as in all poetry, the rhythmic design sensitises us to three things: that there is a pattern to this statement, which continues throughout the poem; that there is a 'poetic' intention; and that ordinary language is being lifted into a specially significant context. A telephone directory is a verbal construction, but it lacks the element of *significant form* shaped by and for a special experience. As J. S. Mill put it, in *What is Poetry?* (1859):

> poetry is not in the object, nor in the scientific truth itself, but in the state of mind in which the one and the other may be contemplated .... Poetry is feeling confessing itself in moments of solitude, and embodying itself in symbols which are the nearest possible representatives of the feeling in the exact shape in which it exists in the poet's mind.

Paradoxically, then, Ghose's poem quoted above is a successful statement of the poet's initial failure to find the poetic (verbal) equivalent for an emotional experience.

The poet raids every resource for expression. The English language is public property, but a poem is an attempt to convey the unique and the particular. An extreme, and oft-quoted example is the poem by Lewis Carroll (1832–98) called 'Jabberwocky', which indicates that however extreme the deviation from 'normal' language may be, there is nevertheless an intelligible (though fantastic) world of decipherable meaning and structure. In its first stanza we can infer sufficient grammatical structure and identify the function of words (noun, verb, qualifiers), even though at least a third of them do not appear in any dictionary:

> 'Twas brillig and the slithy toves
>   Did gyre and gimble in the wabe;
> All mimsy were the borogroves,
>   And the mome raths outgrabe.

This example of deviation from normal language use is but an extreme manifestation of a commonplace feature of poetic language. Dylan Thomas (1914–53) begins a poem with the phrase 'A grief ago', as if time could be measured in suffering as well as by the 'normal' devices of clock and calendar. In *Richard II* (V.5.49–58) by William Shakespeare (1564–1616) the King similarly remarks:

> I wasted time, and now doth time waste me;
> For now hath time made me his numbering clock:
> My thoughts are minutes...
>   ... so sighs and tears and groans
> Show minutes, times, and hours;

In one of the poems in *The Winding Stair* (1933), 'In Memory of Eva
Gore Booth and Con Markiewicz' W. B. Yeats (1865–1939) writes of
'Two girls in silk kimonos, both/Beautiful, one a gazelle'. Dr Johnson
scornfully enquired of one image in the poem 'Obsequies to the Lord
Harrington' (?1613) by John Donne (1571–1631): 'Who but Donne
would have thought that a good man is a telescope?' We might ask the
same sort of question about Wallace Stevens's (1879–1955) 'Anecdote of
the Jar' (1919), which also endows a humdrum object with a vast
metaphysical significance:

> I placed a jar in Tennessee,
> And round it was, upon a hill.
> It made the slovenly wilderness
> Surround that hill.
>
> The wilderness rose up to it,
> and sprawled around, no longer wild.
> The jar was round upon the ground.
> And tall and of a port in air.
>
> It took dominion everywhere.
> The jar was gray and bare.
> It did not give of bird or bush,
> Like nothing else in Tennessee.

The object itself is insignificant, but it is transformed through its focal
ordering of the otherwise shapeless landscape around it and becomes an
image of art itself, imposing order on chaos. Its significance and its value
lie in its relationship (perceived by the poet) to the world around it. Like
a poem, the jar is inanimate, fixed, dumb, until the moment it comes
alive in the landscape of the poet's mind. The poem thus fixes a moment
of meaning in the way that the Anglo-Irish poet Louis MacNeice
(1907–63) described the sonnet, as 'A small eternity', or in the way that
W. H. Auden (1907–73) in his poem 'In Memory of W. B. Yeats'
describes poetry as 'A way of happening, a mouth'. It is not the object
itself, whether it be a world, a girl, a telescope, or a jar, that is significant,
but what the poet sees when he uses these images as bridges into another
territory of experience. Like the cathedral spire in the novel by William
Golding (*b.*1911), *The Spire* (1964), the building which is the poem
organises life around it:

> the tower was laying a hand on the whole landscape, altering it,
> dominating it, enforcing a pattern that reached wherever the tower
> could be seen, by sheer force of its being there.

Reading a poem

A printed poem appeals primarily to our eyes, a poem which is heard to our ears. Ideally, a poem should be read aloud, or 'performed' by the reader in order to activate both senses. To a native speaker, the English words of a poem, like its grammar and syntax, will be familiar, but the *combination* of words, syntax and grammar into a distinct plan requires a suspension of conventional patterns of expectation until the poem establishes its own. The best introduction to poetry is through wide and detailed experience of many poems, and much of the more technical aspects of poetic structure and method will not come into play until prior questions about meaning have been answered. Within the concept of *meaning* in poetry we might discern three main components: *space*, *time*, and *sound*.

Space

The following diagram has no discernible meaning, although it may perhaps suggest the outline of a stool, a table, or any number of similar objects:

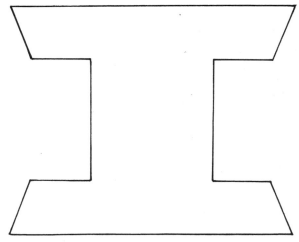

If this abstract space is occupied with particular words, there is the possibility of linking the *content* of an utterance to its physical shape. Words usually bear no relationship whatsoever to the objects they describe (the exceptions being onomatopoeic words which imitate the sound denoted), but here the entire poem, George Herbert's (1593–1633) 'The Altar', has been deliberately set out by the poet to represent in visual terms the central image:

A broken A L T A R, Lord, thy servant reares,
Made of a heart, and cemented with teares:
Whose parts are as thy hand did frame;
No workmans tool hath touch'd the same.
A   H E A R T   alone
Is   such   a   stone,
As   nothing   but
Thy pow'r doth cut.
Wherefore each part
Of my hard heart
Meets in this‾frame,
To praise thy name:
That if I chance to hold my peace,
These stones to praise thee may not cease.
O   let   thy   blessed   S A C R I F I C E   be   mine,
And   sanctifie   this   A L T A R   to   be   thine.

There are numerous additional examples of this poem-in-space technique, such as Herbert's 'Easter Wings', and Robert Herrick's (1591–1674) 'The Pillar of Fame', and each poet has in common attempted to make language into a form of sculpture, an eccentric though ingenious transference. The crucial point to appreciate, however, is that there is no relationship here between words and shape as such. It is only because of the *word* ALTAR that the visual shape has acquired a (decorative) significance. This may easily be demonstrated if we substitute another two-syllable word instead of it (for instance, hymn-book), in which case there would be no spatial significance at all.

Time

Just as the shape of a poem cannot exist independently of its verbal meaning, *rhythm* is meaningless in poetry without reference to verbal meaning. An example constructed by the literary critic I. A. Richards in 1929 shows that we can create the approximate rhythmic shape of a poem in virtually nonsensical language to indicate this:

J. Drootan-Sussting Benn
Mill-down Leduren N.
   Telamba-taras oderwainto weiring
Awersey zet bidreen
Ownd istellester sween
   Lithabian tweet ablissood owdswown stiering
Apleven aswetsen sestinal
Yintomen I adaits afurf I gallas Ball.*

* See I. A. Richards, *Practical Criticism: A Study of Literary Judgment*, Routledge & Kegan Paul, London, 1929, p. 232.

The 'real' as opposed to 'dummy', stanza of which this is a rhythmic phantom is stanza fifteen of John Milton's (1608–74) 'On the Morning of Christ's Nativity' (1629):

Yea, Truth and Justice then
Will down return to men,
    Orb'd in a Rain-bow; and like glories wearing
Mercy will sit between,
Thron'd in Celestial sheen,
    With radiant feet the tissued clouds down steering,
And Heav'n as at some Festivall
Will open wide the Gates of her high Palace wall.

Clearly, we can talk about the 'rhythmic qualities' in so far as they support meaning, or mood, or tone in the Milton stanza, but not in the case of its rhythmic dummy, which is meaningless.

Sound

In spite of what has been said about the arbitrary relationship between rhythm and meaning unless meaning *indicates* a link, some poems elaborate sound and rhythmic considerations above all others. Here is Percy Bysshe Shelley's (1792–1822) 'A Lament' (1824):

O world! O life! O time!
On whose last steps I climb,
    Trembling at that where I had stood before;
When will return the glory of your prime?
    No more – Oh, never more!

Out of the day and night
A joy has taken flight;
    Fresh spring, and summer, and winter hoar
Move my faint heart with grief, but with delight
    No more – Oh, never more!

The *first stage* of this poem's composition shows Shelley's search for an appropriate lyric shape and sound as a more urgent priority than words:

Ah time, oh night, oh day
~~Ni nal ni na, na ni~~
~~Ni na ni na, ni na~~
Oh life O death, O time
    Time a di
~~Never Time~~
Ah time, a time O-time
  ~~Time!~~

The *second stage* seems to have found its words, but lost its shape:

Oh time, oh night oh day
~~A day oh night, alas~~
   ~~O~~ Death time night oh
Oh, Time
Oh time o night oh day

In the *third stage* Shelley seems to have hammered out the metrical shape of the first stanza without words at all, but having achieved the desired sound-shape proceeded to fill it with words:

<table>
<tr><td align="center">(1)</td><td align="center">(2)</td></tr>
<tr><td>

Na na, na na na na
Nă nă na na na – nă nă
  Nă nă nă nă nā nā
Na na nā nā nâ ă na

Na na na – nă nă – na na
  Na na na na – na na na
    [na na
Na na na na na
  Na na
Na na na na na
  Na na
Na na na na na na!

</td><td>

Oh time, oh night, o day alas
O day ~~serenest~~, o day
O day alas the day
That thou shouldst sleep when we
    [awake to say

O time time – o death – o day
O day, o death for life is far from
    [thee
O thou wert never free
For death is now with thee
~~And life is far from~~
O death, o day for life is far from thee

</td></tr>
</table>

What this poem-in-progress shows, of course, is the *integration* of sound, shape, and lyric structure until a fusion of all elements is achieved*. Before looking at a poem which illustrates this intense integration of parts with meaning, one brief example is necessary to highlight the arbitrary relationship between sound and meaning. In *The Princess* (1850), by Alfred Lord Tennyson (1809–92) there is this:

The moan of doves in immemorial elms,
And murmur of innumerable bees.

The American poet John Crowe Ransom (1888–1974) parodied the second line as 'the murdering of innumerable beeves'. Nobody would deny that Tennyson's line creates in sound the actual noise made by bees, but equally, a similar sound-sense relationship in Ransom's line 'means' nothing at all. If we hear a meaning in a sound, it is the context which sensitises us to the possibility, not the individual sound. Meanings are attached to words by convention. Even so, words do not exist in a

---

* For further discussion of Shelley's process of composition, see H. Buxton Forman, *Note Books of Percy Bysshe Shelley*, 3 vols, St Louis, 1911.

lexicographical vacuum: they come with associations already attached by previous usage. As Ezra Pound pointed out, alluding to a speech in Shakespeare's *Macbeth*, 'You can hardly say 'incarnadine' without one or more of your auditors thinking of a particular line of verse.'*

So far, we have been attempting to separate out the components of poetry in terms of its spatial, temporal and sonic dimensions. The ultimate aim of a poet, however, is to integrate all of these elements in order to produce a verbal statement in which everything from overall shape to individual word-choice is organically related in the most precise way possible. A poem *denies* the arbitrariness of language and provides us with the illusion of uniqueness. This claim may be tested on 'Inversnaid' (1881; published 1918), by Gerard Manley Hopkins (1844–89):

> This darksome burn, horseback brown, 1
> His rollrock highroad roaring down,
> In coop and in comb the fleece of his foam
> Flutes and low to the lake falls home.
>
> A windpuff-bonnet of fáwn-fróth 5
> Turns and twindles over the broth
> Of a pool so pitchblack, féll-frówning,
> It rounds and rounds Despair to drowning.
>
> Degged with dew, dappled with dew
> Are the groins of the braes that the brook treads through. 10
> Wiry heathpacks, flitches of fern,
> And the beadbonny ash that sits over the burn.
>
> What would the world be, once bereft
> Of wet and of wildness? Let them be left.
> O let them be left, wildness and wet; 15
> Long live the weeds and the wilderness yet.

Our immediate sense of a visual pattern (four stanzas) is everywhere endorsed by rhythmic and sound patterning. A four-stress line (marked by the poet himself in lines 5 and 7), with a varying number of relatively unstressed syllables (compare line 1 with line 11) is structurally unified by alliteration (coop/comb; *f*leece/*f*oam), terminal rhyme (froth/broth) and internal rhyme (comb/foam in line 3), and assonance (rollrock/highroad; comb/foam, in lines 2 and 3). In the first stanza the subject

---

* Ezra Pound, *ABC of Reading*, Faber & Faber, London, 1951, p. 37. See *Macbeth*, II.2.61–4:

> Will all great Neptune's ocean wash this blood
> Clean from my hand? No, this my hand will rather
> The multitudinous seas incarnadine,
> Making the green one red.

('darksome burn') does not meet its main verb ('falls home') until the last possible moment, thus providing in the syntax itself the impression of movement through time. 'Twindles' in line 6 will not be found in a dictionary in the sense implied here, but seems to combine 'twist' and 'dwindle'. Nor will 'beadbonny', although its meaning (beautified by its bead-like buds) is clear enough.

Hopkins celebrates the untrammelled energy of natural fertility in the wilderness through a poem which *deviates* from conventional order in its word-choice, syntax, rhythm and grammar (is 'Flutes' in the fourth line a noun or a verb, or both at once?). This poem creates originality of form and expression in order to capture uniqueness of experience. It is an image in words of its total meaning, and illustrates very precisely the kind of integral relationship between form and content which we look for in all successful poetry.

Chapter 2

Rhythm and rhyme

Metre: some definitions

'There is no escape from metre; there is only mastery.'

(T. S. Eliot)

I put my hat upon my head
And walked into the Strand,
And there I met another man
Whose hat was in his hand.

(Samuel Johnson)

Johnson's little parody indicates that perfection of metrical form as form is no guarantee of literary excellence. But what *is* metre? Walking, breathing, singing, night and day, the months and years, seasons and generations, all have rhythm, but only poetry and song have metrical rhythm, that is, the recurrence in a poetic line of regular rhythmic units. Like grammar, metre has rules, but the rules exist as a substructure, a notional system to be exploited, varied, concealed. If regularity is monotonous, then complete absence of pattern may be anarchy. The importance as well as the limitations of metre for an understanding of poetry have been indicated by William K. Wimsatt and Monroe C. Beardsley, influential American critical theorists:

> You can write a grammar of the meter. And if you cannot, there is no meter. But you cannot write a grammar of the meter's interaction with the sense, any more than you can write a grammar of the arrangement of metaphors. The interactions and the metaphors are the free and individual and unpredictable (though not irrational) parts of the poetry. You can perceive them, and study them, and talk about them, but not write rules for them. The meter, like the grammar and the vocabulary, is subject to rules. It is just as important to observe what meter a poem is written in (especially if it is written in one of the precise meters of the syllable-stress tradition) as it is to observe what language the poem is written in.*

* W. K. Wimsatt and Monroe C. Beardsley, 'The Concept of Meter: An Exercise in Abstraction', originally published in 1959, but conveniently found in Harvey Gross, ed., *The Structure of Verse: Modern Essays on Prosody*, Fawcett Publications, New York, 1966, p. 163.

There are three basic types of metre. In Anglo-Saxon poetry we find *accentual metre*, that is, poetry in which the number of syllables but not the number of accents per line is variable. In each half-line of Anglo-Saxon poetry there are always two stressed syllables, thus four syllables are stressed in each verse, as in this extract from *Beowulf*:

> þa waes on héalle heárdecg tógen,
> swéord ofer sétlum, sídran mánig
> háfen hánda faest; hélm ne gemúnde,
> býrnan síde, þe hine se bróga angéat.

Accentual metre did not die out with Anglo-Saxon poetry. Metre based on an equal number of stresses per line, irrespective of an exact number of syllables per stress, is found in ballads, in nursery rhymes, in the poetry of T. S. Eliot (1888–1965), W. H. Auden, and Gerard Manley Hopkins (whose 'sprung rhythm' is a variation of accentual metre: see the section on 'Metrical variation' below).

The second type of metre is *syllabic metre*, in which there is a fixed number of syllables per line but in which the number of accents is variable. Pure syllabic verse resists regular patterns of stressed and unstressed syllables within the verse, as in the Zulfikar Ghose poem quoted in Chapter 1, p. 10 above, or in this example from Thom Gunn's (*b.*1929) *My Sad Captains*, which is a seven-syllable line:

> I am approaching. Past dry
> towers softly seeding from mere
> delicacy of age, I
> penetrate, through thickets, or
> over warm herbs my feet press
> to brief potency. Now with . . .

The third type of metre is a combination of these types, that is *accentual-syllabic*. This type has dominated English poetry for the last four hundred years, and is characterised by a regular pattern in the number of both syllables and stresses in each line. The conventionally agreed notation for recording metrical stress in accentual-syllabic verse is through the use of metrical units called *feet*, i.e. combinations of stressed and unstressed syllables. Obviously, any syllable capable of being uttered is stressed to some extent and therefore variable *degrees* of relative stress are identifiable. There are some limitations in using this descriptive method. Classical metrics was *quantitative* (i.e. the metre depends not on stress but on the 'quantity' or duration of a syllable, and the foot consists of 'long' or 'short' syllables). English has an accentual-syllabic stress system, which means that unlike Latin it cannot make a short syllable long by metrically stressing it, nor can an absence of metrical stress make a long syllable short. Even though we recognise that this is a misapplication of one system to another, its general acceptance and the absence of better schemes require us to use it. There are five basic types of metrical foot:*

iambic foot, or iamb: this consists of an unstressed syllable followed by a stressed syllable, as in *repeat.*

NOTE: there is only one way of saying *repeat*; stress inheres in words themselves, but there is no rhythmic pattern until a sequence of repeated stressed and unstressed syllables is discernible.

trochaic foot, or trochee: a stressed followed by an unstressed syllable, as in *never.*

NOTE: there is only one way of saying *never*, but in a poetic line – for instance, Shakespeare's *King Lear*, V.3.308, 'Never, never, never, never, never' – *degrees* of relative stress would be discernible.

anapestic foot, or anapest: two unstressed syllables followed by a stressed syllable, as in *interrupt.*

dactylic foot, or dactyl: a stressed syllable followed by two unstressed syllables, as in *possible*, or *Washington.*

spondaic foot, or spondee: two successive stressed syllables, as in *heartbreak.*

pyrrhic foot, or pyrrhic; two successive unstressed syllables, as in the middle of the phrase *the top/of the/morning.*

NOTE: the spondee and pyrrhic feet occur only occasionally in English poetry, as variations rather than as standard metric units.

Scansion is the name given to what we do when we read a piece of poetry with the intention of discovering its underlying metrical pattern. The stressed syllable is generally marked by a sign (⁄), and is called the *ictus*, whereas the unstressed syllable is marked (⌣), and is called the *remiss*. A single poetic line is called a *verse*, and different verse lengths are defined in terms of the number and type of poetic feet they contain:

monometer: one foot	*pentameter:* five feet
dimeter: two feet	*hexameter:* six feet (an Alexandrine
trimeter: three feet	is a verse of six iambic feet)
tetrameter: four feet	*heptameter:* seven feet

To describe the metrical components of a verse, two elements need to be defined. Thus Alexander Pope's (1688–1744) line,

And learn to crawl upon poetic feet

has five iambic feet, and is therefore called an iambic pentameter. This rather deadening mechanical procedure will determine the *metrical*

---

* Those poets who have experimented with imitations of Greek and Latin quantitative versification include: Sidney, Spenser, Coleridge, Tennyson, Longfellow and Louis MacNeice. It has never been completely achieved in English, since English depends on *qualitative* stress rather than *quantitative* length. (See Chapter 5, p. 118.)

structure, but it will not tell us how to read, or *perform*, the line. It should be called the norm, or paradigm, from which the actual line in performance will vary. Here is the metrical paradigm of an iambic pentameter line (W = weak stress, S = strong stress):

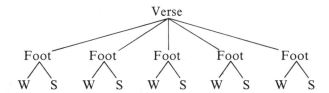

Similar diagrams could be drawn up for other metrical structures, such as trochaic pentameters, anapestic dimeters, and so on.* The point is that actual performance of a line of verse by a sensitive reader will not reconstruct this paradigm, but will mediate between the metrical stress paradigm and the normal rhythms of 'pure stress', or naturalistic speech. The extent of the combination of formal and naturalistic demands is, of course, variable, as is the degree of stress itself. It is this constant tension which provides one strand in the excitement of re-creating a poem in performance. If we return to the line from Pope, its *metrical structure* is this:

And leárn | tŏ cráwl | ŭpón | pŏé | tĭc féet

but its *naturalistic*, or *performance structure* is this:

And leárn | tŏ cráwl | ŭpŏn | pŏé | tĭc féet

The fact that in reading the line we will not fully stress the 'on' in 'upon' does not mean that this line is irregular. If deviation from the absolute norm constituted irregularity, then nearly every line of poetry in English is irregular! What this indicates is that *metrical rules* are here dominated by the rules of natural performance. To read the line otherwise would be ludicrously mechanistic, even if we knew that what Pope is doing here is satirising dull, mechanical poets who follow rules slavishly and without imagination. The *metrical expectation* that the particle 'on' will be stressed is enough to maintain the regular iambic rhythm.

Scansion thus provides an abstract pattern, or metrical paradigm, to which the individual verse bears a fluctuating, love–hate relationship. Nevertheless, perception of the pattern is essential, for it provides distinct controls, and is in fact the only method we can use to define and appreciate variation and error. Why, for example, is the second line of the following couplet, from an *An Essay on Criticism* (1711) by Alexander Pope an inaccurate version of the original?

* See D. A. Reibel and S. A. Schane, eds., *Modern Studies in English*, Holt Rinehart, New Jersey, 1969, particularly 'The Linguistic Basis of English Prosody', pp. 379–94.

> True Wit is Nature to advantage dress'd;
> What was thought, but ne'er so well express'd.

Of the 10,565 lines in Milton's *Paradise Lost* (1674), all but a few are iambic pentameters. Here are two of them:

> Rocks, caves, lakes, fens, bogs, dens, and shades of death
> Immutable, immortal, infinite

The first has eight strong stresses, the second has three, but both have the same inherent pattern of five metric stresses, since the metrical paradigm is iambic pentameter. We can only define this extraordinary skill in variation by first recognising the underlying metrical structure.

The following examples, with the exception of the last two, illustrate iambic metres, arranged in ascending order of frequency. In the first four examples the metrical paradigm is given, followed by the probable performance stress pattern:

1. **Monometer:** Robert Herrick's one-stress iambic lines

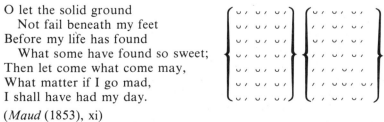

> Thus I
> Pass by
>   And die
> As one,
> Unknown
>   And gone

('Upon his Departure Hence', 1648)

2. **Dimeter:** Michael Drayton's (1563–1631) two-stress iambic lines

> Most good, most fair,
> Or things as rare,
> To call you 's lost;
> For all the cost
> Words can bestow
> So poorly show, ...

('Amouret Anacreontic', c.1600)

3. **Trimeter:** Tennyson's 'Song', three-stress iambic lines

> O let the solid ground
>   Not fail beneath my feet
> Before my life has found
>   What some have found so sweet;
> Then let come what come may,
> What matter if I go mad,
> I shall have had my day.

(*Maud* (1853), xi)

4. **Tetrameter:** Geoffrey Chaucer's (*c*.1340–1400) four-stress iambic lines, or octosyllabic couplets

> I have gret wonder, be this lyght,
> How that I lyve, for day ne nyght
> I may nat slepe wel nygh noght;
> I have so many an ydel thoght,
> Purely for defaute of slep,
> That, by my trouthe, I take no kep
> Of nothing, how hyt cometh or gooth,
> Ne me nys nothyng leef looth.

(*The Book of the Duchess, c.* 1369)

5. **Pentameter:** Dryden's five-stress *rhyming* couplets

> A man so various, that he seem'd to be
> Not one, but all Mankind's Epitome.
> Stiff in Opinions, always in the wrong;
> Was every thing by starts, and nothing long:
> But, in the course of one revolving Moon,
> Was Chymist, Fidler, States-Man, and Buffoon:
> Then all for Women, Painting, Rhiming, Drinking;
> Besides ten thousand freaks that dy'd in thinking.

(*Absalom and Achitophel*, 1681)

or, in the five-stress *unrhymed* iambic line (*blank verse*) of Milton

> A little onward lend thy guiding hand
> To these dark steps, a little further on;
> For yonder bank hath choice of Sun or shade;
> There I am wont to sit, when any chance
> Relieves me from my task of servile toil,
> Daily in the common Prison else enjoined me,
> Where I a Pris'ner chaind, scarce freely draw
> The air imprisond also, close and damp,
> Unwholsom draught: but here I feel amends

(*Samson Agonistes*, 1671)

6. **Hexameter:** Sir Philip Sidney's (1554–86) six-stress iambic line

> Loving in truth, and fain in verse my love to show,
> That She, dear She, might take some pleasure of my pain,
> Pleasure might cause her read, reading might make her know,
> Knowledge might pity win, and pity grace obtain,
> I sought fit words to paint the blackest face of woe;
> Studying inventions fine, her wits to entertain,
> Oft turning others' leaves, to see if thence would flow
> Some fresh and fruitful showers upon my sun-burn'd brain.

But words came halting forth, wanting Inventions stay,
Invention Natures child, fled step-dame Studies blowes,
And others feet still seem'd but strangers in my way.
Thus great with child to speake and helpless in my throes
Biting my trewand pen, beating my selfc for spite,
Foole, said my Muse to me, looke in thy heart and write.

(*Astrophel and Stella* (the first poem in the first of the great
Elizabethan sonnet cycles), 1591)

7. **Heptameter:** Algernon Charles Swinburne's (1837–1909) seven-stress
   anapestic lines

NOTE: in performance these lines tend to break up into a four-stress
followed by a three-stress component in each line.

Come on then, ye dwellers by nature in darkness, and like to the
    leaves' generations,
That are little of might, that are moulded of mire, unenduring and
    shadowlike nations,
Poor plumeless ephemerals, comfortless mortals, as visions of
    creatures fast fleeing,
Lift up your mind unto us that are deathless, and dateless the date of
    our being.

(*The Birds*, from Aristophanes)

8. **Eight-stress line:** Tennyson's *Locksley Hall*, in eight-stress trochaics,

NOTE: this also fails to sustain the integrity of the line, and in
performance becomes two equal half-lines of four stresses each:

Comrades, leave me here a little, while as yet 'tis early morn:
Leave me here, and when you want me, sound upon the bugle-horn.
'Tis the place, and all around it, as of old, the curlews call,
Dreary gleams about the moorland flying over Locksley Hall

(*Locksley Hall*, 1842)

The poems listed above illustrate a fundamental principle of metre,
that it always exists in tension with the 'pure stress' requirements of
naturalistic speech rhythm. There are two implications in this principle:
(1) that poetic metre may tend towards metrical regularity (nursery
rhymes, some of Byron, Shelley, Swinburne, and some narrative poetry,
such as the American poet Henry Wadsworth Longfellow's (1807–82)
Hiawatha (1855), would fall into this category, since domination by the
metrical system means that stresses are placed more or less arbitrarily on
words according to their position in the line); (2) that poetic metre may
tend towards naturalistic utterance (the poetry of John Donne and the
verse of T. S. Eliot's (1888–1965) plays, for example, where the metrical
domination is weak and the naturalistic demands are dominant, that is,

the normal prose rhythms are used). Neither of these two extremes poses any difficulty to the reader, since in metrically dominated poetry we can simply beat out the rhythms and in the second we can read it as though it were prose divided into lengths. There is no qualitative difference between the two, only a difference of function and purpose.

Samuel Butler's (1612–80) *Hudibras* (Part I, 1662) takes a serious subject (Puritan claims to divine revelation) and degrades it by grotesque exaggeration. Here, the thumping rhythms of the metrically dominant octosyllabic rhymed couplets are perfect for the intended effect of satiric deflation:

> He was in logic a great critic,
> Profoundly skilled in analytic.
> He could distinguish and divide
> A hair 'twixt south and southwest side;
> On either which he would dispute,
> Confute, change hands, and still confute.
> He'd undertake to prove, by force
> Of argument, a man's no horse;
> He'd prove a buzzard is no fowl,
> And that a lord may be an owl,
> A calf an alderman, a goose a justice,
> And rooks committee-men and trustees.

The deliberately mechanical quality of the poetry characterises and imprisons Hudibras as a man with a clockwork mind. In a similar, but far more subtle way, Dryden portrays the character Zimri (in example 5 above, p. 24) as a split personality: he is torn apart across and between the juxtapositions of the couplet form. Neither effect is *intrinsic* to the form itself. Milton's *L'Allegro* and *Il Penseroso* (1645) use rhymed octosyllabic couplets, but their effect is totally unlike Butler's use of the same metrical form; and the use of the heroic couplet by both Dryden and Pope is astonishingly versatile. By contrast, the final paragraph of 'Journey of the Magi' (1927) by T. S. Eliot defies a metrically dominated reading: it is of course using a speaking voice and colloquial idiom, but also it is *about* confusion and anxiety. Here is a mind agitated by the birth of Christ, which knows that nothing can ever be the same again:

> All this was a long time ago, I remember,
> And I would do it again, but set down
> This set down
> This: were we led all that way for
> Birth or Death? There was a Birth, certainly,
> We had evidence and no doubt. I had seen birth and death,
> But had thought they were different; this Birth was
> Hard and bitter agony for us, like Death, our death.

Metrical variation

Between the two extremes of metrically dominated poetry and free verse (as in the example by T. S. Eliot) lies the vast majority of English poetry. The poet chooses the most appropriate metrical style as a means of ordering his statement. Obviously, an inappropriate choice could be disastrous: what is merit in a limerick may be disaster in a love-lyric.

There are four formal methods by which a poet may vary the metrical paradigm:

(a) substitution of one or more of the expected feet by an 'irregular' foot;

(b) the addition of any number of unaccented syllables;

(c) varying the position of a caesura (a pause within the line or verse);

(d) the use of end-stopped or run-on lines

Substitution

It is rare for the metrical structure of a line to match exactly the natural rhythm of performance, but it does happen, for example, in the twelfth line of Shakespeare's sonnet XII:

When I do count the clock that tells the time

where the five feet are regularly (though perhaps not equally) iambic; or in *Paradise Lost*, II, 950:

And swims, or sinks, or wades, or creeps, or flyes.

Equally, it is rare for the naturalistic performance to replace the paradigm completely, although the line from *King Lear*, V.3.308, spoken over the dead Cordelia,

Never, never, never, never, never

substitutes a trochee for every one of the five iambs in the paradigm. Except in poetry which is deliberately putting the Muse on the rack (as in satire, burlesque and nursery rhymes) the degree of substitution is strictly controlled. Pope's couplet in *Essay on Criticism*, lines 359–60:

1	2	3	4	5
When A	jax strives	some rock's	vást wéight	to throw,
1	2	3	4	5
The line	too la	bours, and	the words	móve slów;

substitutes in the fourth and fifth feet of the first and second lines respectively a spondee for the 'expected' iamb. The ideas of heaviness and slowness are thereby *metrically* indicated. John Keats (1795–1821) does the same in his 'Ode on a Grecian Urn' (1820):

Thou still unravish'd bride of quietness,
Thou foster-child of silence | and slów tíme |

If the insertion of a spondee adds weight and pause, then a pyrrhic substitution (that is, two successive unstressed syllables) will have the effect of rapidity or grace, as in Pope's lines in *Essay on Criticism*, lines 361–2:

No so when swift Camilla scours the plain,
Flies o'er th'unbending corn, and skims | alŏng | the Main

where an *extra* foot in the fifth position in the second line has the paradoxical effect of speeding up the line.

The substitution of an initial trochaic foot for an iamb, using an active verb, makes a startling and sometimes violent disruptive opening, as in Donne's 'Holy Sonnet XIV':

| Báttĕr | my heart, three person'd God; for you
As yet but knocke, breathe, shine, and seeke to mend;

or, as a modifier, may provide an abrupt focal emphasis, as in Keats's 'On First Looking into Chapman's Homer':

Look'd at each other with a wild surmise –
| Sílĕnt, | upon a peak in Darien

where, in context, and supported by punctuation and syntax, the trochee marks a sudden shift in tone, mood, and direction. Substitution may, of course, occur at any position in the verse, initial, medial, or terminal.

Addition of unaccented syllables

Hopkins's sonnet 'Felix Randal' is built on lines of six strong stresses. What he called 'sprung rhythm' involved 'scanning by accents or stresses alone, without any account of the number of syllables, so that a foot may be one strong syllable or it may be many light and one strong' (Letter to R. W. Dixon, 5 October, 1878). Unaccented extra syllables, called by Hopkins 'outriding feet', are indicated by a sign (⌣):

Félix Rándal the Fárrier, O he is deád then? my dúty all eńded,
Who have watched his moúld of man, big-bóned and hardy-
                                                    [handsome
Píning, píning, till tíme when reáson rambled in it and sóme
Fátal foúr disorders, fléshed there, áll conténded?

Hopkins clearly signals his additional unaccented syllables, but very often a poet will elide an extra syllable in order to preserve the metrical shape, as in the second of these lines from Donne's 'To the Countesse of Bedford':

> I cannot tell them, nor my selfe, nor you,
> But leave, lest truth b'endanger'd by my praise

(The technical term for this method of concealing an extra syllable is *syncope*, and, as Hopkins was aware, Milton was the expert in this particular art.)

Caesural variation

Metrical monotony is assured in a series of lines of verse all exhibiting a medial pause in approximately the same place. This is the intended effect, however, in Canto II lines 7–18 of Pope's *The Rape of the Lock*, where Pope deftly characterises the mental world of Belinda as bland and undifferentiated ritual posturing:

> On her white breast a sparkling cross she wore,
> Which Jews might kiss, ‖ and infidels adore.
> Her lively looks a sprightly mind disclose,
> Quick as her eyes, ‖ and as unfix'd as those:
> Favours to none, ‖ to all she smiles extends;
> Oft she rejects, ‖ but never once offends.
> Bright as the sun, ‖ her eyes the gazers strike,
> And, like the sun, ‖ they shine on all alike.
> Yet graceful ease, ‖ and sweetness void of pride,
> Might hide her faults, ‖ if belles had faults to hide:
> If to her share some female errors fall,
> Look on her face, ‖ and you'll forget 'em all.

Almost without exception, a caesural pause (marked ‖) precedes a line or half-line which flattens the expectation aroused by the complimentary remarks about Belinda. Elsewhere, Pope manipulates the caesura for entirely opposite effects, but again as an element in total meaning. This passage from *The Dunciad* describes a butterfly chase:

> Of all the enamelled race, whose silv'ry wing
> Waves to the tepid zephyrs of the spring,
> Or swims along the fluid atmosphere,
> Once brightest shined this child of heat and air.
> I saw, and started from its vernal bow'r,
> The rising game, and chas'd from flow'r to flow'r.
> It fled, I followed; now in hope, now pain;
> It stopt; I stopt; it moved, I moved again.
> At last it fixed, 'twas on what plant it pleased,
> And where it fixed, the beauteous bird I seized.

In the last six lines the caesura flits across the lines of verse to enact the irregular nature of the pursuit. Ezra Pound described rhythm as 'a form cut into TIME, as a design is determined SPACE', and certainly the use of the caesura can leave the clearest chisel-mark of the poet's shaping art.

In Old English poetry the caesura is predictably medial, as in the line from *Beowulf*,

Ongeat þa se goda ‖ grundwyrgenne

– an inflexible feature of its *prosodic* structure with no real chance of responding to fluctuations in argument and meaning. By contrast, these lines from Milton's *Paradise Lost*,

Thus with the Year
Seasons return, ‖ but not to me returns
Day, ‖ or the sweet approach of Ev'n or Morn
Or sight of vernal bloom, ‖ or Summers Rose

deploy the caesura to reflect meaning. A piquant emphasis on the non-return of day, sunset, sunrise, the colours of spring and summer is not only rhythmically pointed but also an autobiographical fact: Milton was blind when he wrote these lines.

End-stopped and run-on lines

All of the three methods of metrical variation mentioned so far affect the individual verse. Both options in this section affect the relationship *between* verses. If the natural pause at the end of a line of verse coincides with the end of a phrase, clause, or sentence, the verse is *end-stopped*. If the sense requires no terminal pause, it is a *run-on line* (otherwise known as *enjambement*). In the last example from Pope above ('Of all the enamelled race . . .'), all but the first and last lines are end-stopped lines. Keats's *Endymion* (I, 89–93), on the other hand, offers an effective example of run-on lines:

Full in the middle of this pleasantness
There stood a marble altar, with a tress
Of flowers budded newly; and the dew
Had taken fairy fantasies to strew
Daisies upon the sacred sward . . .

The regular iambic rhythm of these lines provides a coherence which the sentence and syntax override. For a more arbitrary relationship (where every expectation of conventional syntax is subjugated to the demands of the verse line), there is no better example than the opening lines of Hopkins's 'The Windhover':

> I caught this morning morning's minion, king-
> dom of daylight's dauphin, dapple-dawn-drawn Falcon, in
> his riding
> Of the rolling level underneath him steady air, and striding
> High there, how he rung upon the rein of a wimpling wing
> In his ecstasy! then off, off forth on swing,
> As a skate's heel sweeps smooth on a bow-bend: the hurl
> and gliding
> Rebuffed the big wind. My heart in hiding
> Stirred for a bird, – the achieve of, the mastery of the thing!

Only one line (the sixth) permits a terminal pause to coincide with natural syntax, and every other line cascades into the next like a swooping bird of prey. Almost accidentally, it seems, every line ending rhymes with all the others.

Rough and smooth poetry

As a general principle, metre requires a high degree of ordering from language, whereas the poet will demand that language be as flexible as possible in order to accommodate his particular voice. Eighteenth-century English poetry adopted the metrical form of the iambic pentameter; its theoretical attraction lay in its close approximation to the rhythms of ordinary speech, or, to put it another way, it was thought to be as free as necessary from *metrical domination*. The poetry of John Donne was thought to be excessively 'rough'. To us there is a dramatic immediacy and a permanent intellectual toughness in much of Donne's poetry precisely because of its craggy shape. It is not that Donne's rhymes are awkward, or that his lines do not scan properly, but that any attempt to read the lines metrically is severely disrupted by their naturalistic style, particularly his use of disjunctive pauses, where we might feel that the poet has done too little work organising the language towards the metre, and the reader has to do too much:

> On a huge hill,
> Cragged, and steep, Truth stands, and hee that will
> Reach her, about must, and about must goe;
> And what the hills suddennes resists, winne so;
> Yet strive so, that before age, deaths twilight,
> Thy Soule rest, for none can worke in that night.
> To will, implyes delay, therefore now doe:
> Hard deeds, the bodies paines; hard knowledge too
> The mindes indeavours reach, and mysteries
> Are like the Sunne, dazzling, yet plaine to all eyes.
>
> ('Satyre III', lines 79–88)

Donne perceived most things through the spectacles of paradox, and his religious poetry is often a history of tortured hope and bleak despair. However, when mellifluousness (or 'smoothness') is required, few poets equal Donne:

> Sweetest love, I do not goe,
>   For weariness of thee,
> Nor in hope the world can show
>   A fitter love for mee;
>   But since that I
> Must dye at last, 'tis best,
> To use my selfe in jest
>   Thus by fain'd deaths to dye.   ('Song')

Dr Johnson felt that blank verse, that is unrhymed iambic pentameter, ran the danger of too much naturalness and too little metricality. This preference for metrically shaped utterance underpinned his feeling that Milton's blank verse was monotonous:

> The musick of the English heroick line strikes the ear so faintly that it is easily lost unless all the syllables of every line co-operate together: this co-operation can only be obtained by the preservation of every verse unmingled with another, as a distinct system of sounds: and this distinctness is obtained and preserved by the artifice of rhyme.*

Never the man to practise one thing and preach another, Johnson shaped his own poetry into neatly ordered, end-stopped, and perfectly rhymed couplets:

> Let Observation with extensive View,
> Survey Mankind from China to Peru;
> Remark each anxious Toil, each eager Strife,
> And watch the busy Scenes of crouded Life;
> Then say how Hope and Fear, Desire and Hate,
> *O'erspread* with Snares the clouded Maze of Fate,
> Where *wav'ring* Man, *betray'd* by *vent'rous* Pride,
> To tread the dreary Paths without a Guide.
>   ('The Vanity of Human Wishes')

The four words italicised by the present author in the passage above indicate a further preference: the *metrical* system demands ten syllables, thus the naturalistic reading is compacted to fit it. The adjustment is needed not only to make the lines regular, but also to make the lines 'smooth'. John Donne would have left the adjustment to the reader, whereas Byron (and satirical verse in general) may insist on every metrical item being given its full value. In Butler's *Hudibras* this is most

---

* Samuel Johnson, 'Life of Milton', in *Lives of the Poets* (1779–81).

clearly seen in the rhymes: 'fish up/Bishop', 'philosopher/Ross over', 'KEPLER/people her'; and in Swift's poetry there is 'Neck fast/ Breakfast', 'Journal/Return all', 'a louse old/Household', 'Appearance /a Year Rents', and so on. An anonymous commentator in 1698 made the precise point about the way satirical verse tyrannises over language in order to enforce its metricality:

> to Ridicule, Flatter, Huff, and Banter, by turns; to Scratch and Claw now, and anon to Grin and Bite like a Satyr .... It is wonderful to traverse its Arbitrary Power, how it proceeds without regard to *Periods*, *Colons*, or *Comma's*: How some times it will change *Accents* for the sake of Rhyme, and, according to the most vulgar and careless Pronunciation, leave out what *Consonants* it pleases. It will end the Verse with a *Preposition*, and make Interjections at its own Libitum. It often uses Grammar so ill, that it will baulk Orthography it self, rather than not assert its own Prerogative.

Judgments on the 'roughness' or 'smoothness' of poetry are thus implicit comments on the extent to which either metricality or naturalistic demands are met.

Free verse

In free verse we can have no call on the structural devices of 'accentual-syllabic' poetry, for it is not capable of division into regular numbers of stressed and unstressed syllables, and has no intrinsically regular rhythm, line-length, or stanzaic forms. This is part of its attraction for the poet who wishes to dispose of all inherited forms and modes of expression and to strike out on his own. Free verse can follow the shape of an utterance, the movement of a thought, and the pursuit of an idea, with total freedom from metrical control.

Or so it seems. In practice, good free verse differs from accentual-syllabic verse in dispensing with a regular metric pattern and rhyme, but nevertheless uses rhythmic patterns of a shadowy kind which recall its rejected antecedents. The poet and critic G. S. Fraser provides an attractive 'definition' of free verse:

> What I recognise as good free verse is verse which does not scan regularly but seems always on the verge of scanning regularly; which is neither strictly in pure stress metre, nor stress syllable metre, not quantitative metre, nor pure syllabics, but which often seems to be getting near to one or other of these, perhaps attempting to fuse two of them, perhaps deliberately and abruptly alternating between one and the other.*

* G. S. Fraser, *Metre, Rhyme and Free Verse*, Methuen, London and New York, 1970, p. 74.

Ordinary prose and colloquial speech are both inherently rhythmical. Évery séntĕnce Ĭ speák măy bĕ stréss-márked.

And as in colloquial speech, the implication of free verse is that stress-rhythms and sentence lengths will sing their *own* individual tunes. There is no point at all in taking up a hostile attitude to free verse as such: that would be as absurd as insisting on only one acceptable dialect of English itself. Certainly, it can produce extraordinarily successful poems. For example, the third stanza of 'Snake' (1923) by the novelist and poet D. H. Lawrence (1885–1930), includes free-verse rhythms which seem to enact the precise, sinuous movement of the reptile it describes:

> He reached down from a fissure in the earth-wall in the gloom
> And trailed his yellow-brown slackness soft-bellied down, over
>   the edge of the stone trough
> And rested his throat upon the stone bottom.

Though there is no predictable and regular metrical scheme here, there is certainly *rhythm*. If there were no rhythm, we would not be able (as we certainly are) to feel as well as see that the 'yellow-brown slackness soft-bellied down' is a compact physical and mobile image of colour moving through space. The real excellence of this image is its *synaesthetic* quality, combining simultaneously ideas of colour, shape, texture and movement. The line-length is a minor factor. After all, Pope achieves the same *effect* of movement in

> A needless Alexandrine ends the song,
> That, like a wounded snake, drags its slow length along.
> (*Essay on Criticism*, lines 356–7)

A contemporary poet, Douglas Dunn, has described free verse as 'the most crucial problem in contemporary British poetry'. He cites the opinion of an influential American poet and critic Yvor Winters (1900–68) that 'the nature of free verse is a permanent obstacle' to 'complexity and profundity', and then asserts that 'poetry does not necessarily inhere in its forms, but in the imagination which uses language and forms'. Dunn then quotes his own poem 'A Removal from Terry Street':

> On a squeaking cart, they push the usual stuff,
> A mattress, bed ends, cups, carpets, chairs,
> Four paperback westerns. Two whistling youths
> In surplus U.S. Army battle-jackets
> Remove their sister's goods. Her husband
> Follows, carrying on his shoulders the son
> Whose mischief we are glad to see removed,
> And pushing, of all things, a lawnmower.

There is no grass in Terry Street. The worms
Come up in cracks in concrete yards in moonlight.
That man, I wish him well. I wish him grass.

This is free verse. But its rhythmic qualities are perched on the edge of *blank verse*. Perhaps only one line (the last) has six strong stresses, and none of the others has fewer than four strong stresses. Lines one, two, four, eight, nine and ten each have five stresses. The pentameter line is thus a shadowy metrical norm. Dunn himself makes this clear:

Technically, the lines are formed by flattening iambic pentameters. Some lines, several phrases and parts of lines are precisely iambic; but the impulse of the poem is descriptive, and I suppose it was the weight of observation and narrative and the presence of people and objects – 'Four paperback westerns' and 'Two whistling youths' – which made it unnatural or undesirable to sustain the iambic rhythm of the classic English line throughout.*

If a poet attempts to secede completely from the old rhythmic forms, to announce, as it were, a Universal Declaration of Metrical Independence, then free verse is a natural choice, for its ability to fuse language and movement is limitless. e.e. cummings's (1894–1962) poem 'she being Brand', about the first drive in a new car, exemplifies this intense fusion of form, rhythm and meaning. Yet its success depends on all manner of syntactic, lexical and grammatical distortions. Here are the last few lines:

                    (it
was the first ride and believe i we was
happy to see how nice she acted right up to
the last minute coming back down by the Public
Gardens i slammed on
the
internalexpanding
&
externalcontracting
brakes Bothatonce and
brought allof her tremB
-ling
to a : dead
stand-
; Still)

The exhilaration of uncertain control of a machine in motion and at speed is conveyed by fluctuating rhythms, totally unpredictable line-

* See P. R. King, *Nine Contemporary Poets: A Critical Introduction*, Methuen, 1979, pp. 223–4.

lengths, bizarre arrangement of grammatical markers (such as punctuation and capitalisation), phrasal disjunctions (disjointed phrases), and so on. The form and the experience are inextricable. The poet's pen and the reader's eye follow movement through space and time in a completely synaesthetic journey. The unconventional becomes the norm. The poetry of cummings differs only in degree (though a large degree) from the poetry of Hopkins in the demands it makes on the reader's willingness and ability to adjust to deviation. Above everything else, however, it should not be thought that eccentricity or egocentricity of form necessarily involve greater 'sincerity' or 'originality' of thought. The poet chooses the most appropriate form for a variety of needs. W. B. Yeats, for example, believed that genuine freedom was only possible for him within the traditional stanza form, and that to choose free verse would compromise both his artistic integrity and a need for emotional reticence:

> It was a long time before I had made a language to my liking; I began to make it when I discovered some twenty years ago that I must seek, not as Wordsworth thought, words in common use, but a powerful and passionate syntax, and a complete coincidence between period and stanza. Because I need a passionate syntax for passionate subject-matter I compel myself to accept those traditional metres that have developed with the language. Ezra Pound, Turner, Lawrence wrote admirable free verse, I could not. I would lose myself, become joyless . . . If I wrote of personal love or sorrow in free verse, or in any rhythm that left it unchanged, amid all its accidence, I would be full of self-contempt because of egotism and indiscretion, and foresee the boredom of my reader. I must choose a traditional stanza, even what I alter must seem traditional. I commit my emotion to shepherds, herdsmen, camel-drivers, learned men, Milton's or Shelley's Platonist, that tower Palmer drew. Talk to me of originality and I will turn on you with rage.*

Rhyme

If all else fails, a poet can make his poem look and sound like a poem by using rhymes. Most things do fail in the verse of William McGonagall (1830–1902), a Scottish writer whose struggle to turn prose thought into poetry resulted in some of the best known bad verse. He never misses a rhyme. Even in poetry of great merit and seriousness the demands of a rhyme scheme may sometimes mangle sense, as in Hopkins's rhyme 'boon he on/Communion' in 'The Bugler's Last Communion'. This

* W. B. Yeats, 'A General Introduction for my Work', *Essays and Introductions*, Macmillan, London, 1961, pp. 521–2.

kind of rhyme would not be out of place in Lord Byron's (1788–1824) *satirical* verse, which uses excessively prominent rhymes such as 'liberal/gibber all' (*Don Juan*, XII, v) in order to mock. Rhyme's function is not exhausted when the formal demands of a poem are met: it also relates to meaning.

But what is rhyme? The *Concise Oxford Dictionary* defines it as 'Identity of sound between words or verse-lines extending from the end to the last fully accented vowel *and not further*' (present author's italics). Rhyme cannot be defined with reference to words, but to what the linguist Geoffrey N. Leech has called 'the final measure of one word [which] rhymes with that of another'.* Thus *greed/agreed* is not, strictly, a rhyme but a complete duplication of sound. Neither is rhyme based necessarily on identity of spelling. Pronunciation is the essence: thus *great* rhymes with *mate*, whereas *bough* and *though* do not. *Great* and *meat* are similar only in the sense that they look alike, and are therefore called *eye-rhymes*. But in earlier poetry, as in Pope's rhyme on Queen Anne in *The Rape of the Lock*

> Here thou, great ANNA! whom three realms obey,
> Does sometimes counsel take – and sometimes tea

the terminal rhyme was at the time of writing a true rhyme. Pronunciation changes, but one might argue here that the awkwardness of this rhyme to us only underlines the bathos intended.

Rhyme is only one aspect of sound-parallelism. Leech points out that the general structural formula for the English syllable is a *cluster of up to three consonants followed by a vowel nucleus of up to four consonants*, i.e. $(C^{0-3}VC^{0-4})$. If all these components of the syllable vary at once, or if they all stay the same, there is no parallelism. There are six possible ways in which variation leading to approved parallelism (or rhyming effect) may occur. In the following list C equals consonant cluster, V equals vowel nucleus:

(a)	C̲VC	great	/ g̲row	s̲end	/ s̲it	(alliteration)
(b)	CV̲C	gr̲e̲at	/ f̲a̲il	s̲e̲nd	/ b̲e̲ll	(assonance)
(c)	CV̲C̲	grea̲t̲	/ mea̲t̲	sen̲d̲	/ han̲d̲	(consonance)
(d)	C̲V̲C	g̲r̲eat	/ g̲r̲azed	s̲e̲nd	/ s̲e̲ll	(reverse rhyme)
(e)	C̲VC̲	g̲rea̲t	/ g̲roa̲t	s̲en̲d̲	/ s̲oun̲d̲	(pararhyme)
(f)	CV̲C̲	gr̲e̲a̲t̲	/ b̲a̲i̲t̲	s̲e̲n̲d̲	/ e̲n̲d̲	(rhyme)

In its earliest historical form, that is, alliteration, the sound-parallelism of Old English verse functions to unite the two half-lines into a verse-unit. A modern imitation of this is found in W. H. Auden's poem 'The Age of Anxiety' (1946):

---

* Geoffrey N. Leech, *A Linguistic Guide to English Poetry*, Longman, London, 1969, p. 91. This is also the source of the list of sound parallelisms below (from *op. cit.*, p. 89).

All war's woes: I can well imagine.
Gun-barrels, gathered in ambush
Mayhem among mountains: minerals break
In by order: on intimate groups of
Tender tissues: at their tough visit

In the poetry of John Skelton (c.1460–1529) the two half-lines of the Old English dimeter verse are separated into two-stress lines linked by terminal rhyme, as in 'Upon a Dead Man's Hand' (c.1498):

But grant us grace
To see thy face
And to purchase
Thine heavenly place,
And thy palace,
Full of solace,
Above the sky
That is so high:
Eternally
To behold and see
The Trinity!

This rhythmically simple poem has a complex array of rhyming features or sound parallelism: alliteration within the line (grant/grace), rhyme across six lines (grace, face, purchase, place, palace, solace), a couplet rhyme (sky, high) and a triplet rhyme (eternally, see, Trinity). The metrical pungency of the poem is determined not only by its incantatory, or prayer-like regular stress-patterns, but also by its predominant use of *masculine rhymes* (a rhyme on a single and terminal syllable). *Feminine rhyme* is a rhyme which includes an unaccented syllable following the accented syllable, as, for example, in 'grinning/brinning' earlier in the same poem.

Though terminal 'true rhyme' is the most obvious example of sound-parallelism, providing a sense of aesthetic shape and also contributing to meaning (in the Pope example above, is politics as much a social ritual for Queen Anne as drinking tea?), there are several additional forms of rhyme:

internal rhyme: as in *The Rime of the Ancient Mariner* (1798) by Samuel Taylor Coleridge (1772–1834) line 381:

'The sails at *noon* left off their *tune*'

reverse rhyme: as in Hopkins's 'Binsey Poplars':

My aspens dear, whose airy cages quelled,
Quelled or quenched in leaves the leaping sun,
All felled, felled, are all felled

pararhyme: as in Wilfred Owen's (1893–1918) 'Strange Meeting' (1920):

It seemed that out of battle I e*scaped*
Down some profound dull tunnel, long since *scooped*
Through granites which titanic wars had *groined.*
Yet also there encumbered sleepers *groaned*

half-rhyme: (consonance in the list on p. 37) as in W. B. Yeats's 'Easter 1916':

I have met them at close of day
Coming with vivid *faces*
From counter or desk among grey
Eighteenth-century *houses.*

Elaborate combinations of sound-parallelism are possible (though not always successful), as in Wilfred Owen's diary fragment for July 1914, which combines an initial half-rhyme with terminal rhyme and various internal sound parallelisms:

⎧ *Leaves*
⎨ *M*urmuring by *m*yriads in the shimmering trees. (*alliteration*)
⎩ *Lives*
    *W*akening with *w*onder in the Pyrenees. (*alliteration*)
⎧ *Birds*
⎨ *Ch*eerily *ch*IRping in the EARly day. (*assonance*)
⎩ *Bards*
    Singing of summer *scything* thro' the hay (*pararhyme and alliteration*)

Above the level of the verse, rhyme is one of the fundamental building-blocks for stanzaic organisation. An entire genre, the sonnet, can be described in terms of its rhyme scheme (see Chapter 3, p. 42–8, below). Rhyme is also a rhythmic marker, a phonetic element in the total design of a line-group or a whole poem. If, as in the case of metrical domination, rhyme ceases to be a support and becomes the whole method of control, ludicrous effects (whether intentional or not) may be achieved. Equally, if there is excessive concentration on any single phonetic device, the sense may be distorted and seriousness sacrificed. In Shakespeare's *A Midsummer Night's Dream*, V.1.144–7, Quince tries too hard in attempting to illustrate in words the (melodramatic) qualities of his knockabout play. The problem here is excessive alliteration, though the comic effect is intentional:

Anon comes Pyramus, sweet youth and tall,
And finds his trusty Thisby's mantle slain:
Whereat, with blade, with bloody blameful blade,
He bravely broach'd his boiling bloody breast.

Chapter 3

Poetic form and thematic shape

Poetic form

The disposition of lines into groups takes us above the level of the individual verse into two categories: *stichic* poetry, in which verse follows verse, as in Milton's *Paradise Lost*, Wordsworth's *The Prelude*, and Shakespeare's *King Lear*; and *strophic* poetry, where we encounter groups of lines (or stanzas), as in Spenser's *The Faerie Queene*, Coleridge's *Ancient Mariner*, and Keats's 'Ode to Autumn'. A poet choosing the stichic form may be writing at great length (*The Prelude*), or for the theatre (*King Lear*), and the poet choosing the strophic form may be writing more briefly and perhaps more intensely. The former will encounter decisions such as whether to use rhyme or not, run-on or end-stopped lines, or both, and caesural variation. The latter may have many of these decisions made for him by the nature of the form chosen. Length has some bearing on the texture of a poem, though, for example, Pope's use of self-contained, end-stopped couplets in the lengthy *Dunciad* or *Essay on Man* is no more prominent than in his shorter poetry. In *Paradise Lost*, however, Milton thinks and writes in paragraphs of verse for which intricate rhyme patterning would be unsuitable. Beyond the paragraph and below the Book, there is no formal subdivision in any of these works. The sonnet, at the other extreme, is strophic in form, and is the outstanding example of the stanza's potential for densely organised and finely turned statement.

Three quarters of English poetry is written in blank verse, that is, stichic form. In the middle period of English (from 1100 to 1500) the four-stress accentual line of Old English poetry is gradually abandoned in favour of syllabic numeration. The two half-lines (or hemistiches) remain in the medieval ballad stanza, with alternating four- and three-stress lines, but now in competition with strophic construction, as in *Sir Gawayne and the Grene Knight* (*c*.1375–1400). The early modern period (from about 1500 to the end of the seventeenth century) sees an increasing imitation of classical literary forms as well as critical discussions in English about metrical matters and rhetoric (as in George Puttenham's *Arte of English Poesie*, 1589, and Dryden's *Essay of Dramatick Poesie*, 1668). The poetry of Sir Philip Sidney, Edmund Spenser (1552–99) and Thomas Campion (1567–1620) is strophic and also imitates the heroic hexameter of Greek lyric. In drama, the iambic

pentameter becomes the staple line, as in Christopher Marlowe
(1564–93) and William Shakespeare. As we have seen, eighteenth-
century poetry was strongly motivated towards metrical regularity:
Pope *versified* Donne's satires, as if in direct response to Dryden's
remark, 'Would not Donne's *Satires*, which abound with so much wit,
appear more charming, if he had taken care of his words, and of his
numbers?' Free verse emerged in the nineteenth century, and Yeats
returned to the staple system of English poetry for the last four hundred
years, accentual syllabism.

Stanza forms evolve as one item in the evolution of poetic styles: all
forms are available to the modern poet and are determined by the
rhythmic mode chosen, the number of feet per line, and the number of
lines. Since Pope, few poets have achieved such mastery in the
pentameter couplet, but Auden's example shows that the Old English
line is still serviceable. The twentieth-century poet is largely free from the
assumption that a particular *form* is required for a particular content.

The stanza forms determined by numbers of lines are:

Couplet: two-line stanzas, as in Alfred Lord Tennyson's *Locksley Hall*
(1842), Wallace Stevens's 'The Man with the Blue Guitar' (1937),
Ogden Nash's 'Tableau at Twilight' (1950), and Thom Gunn's 'Moly'
(1971);

Tercet: three-line stanzas, appearing most frequently as components in
larger units, but found in Robert Herrick's 'Upon Julia's Clothes'
(1648), Percy Bysshe Shelley's 'The Triumph of Life' (1824), Robert
Graves's 'The Straw' (1951) and Seamus Heaney's 'Mid-term Break'
(1969);
NOTE: in Shelley's 'Ode to the West Wind', the tercets are interlaced,
aba bcb cdc, so that the stanza consists of a set of four tercets, closed
by a couplet rhyming with the middle line of the preceding tercet: *aba
bcb cdc ded ee*. This interlaced tercet form is know as *terza rima.*

Quatrain: this four-line grouping is the most common in both European
and American poetry: examples include Thomas Gray's 'Elegy
Written in a Country Churchyard' (1750) (in *heroic quatrains*),
Robert Burns's 'A Red Red Rose' (1796), William Blake's 'The Tyger'
(1794), Alfred Lord Tennyson's 'In Memoriam' (1850), A. E.
Housman's 'On Wenlock Edge' (1896), W. H. Auden's 'Spain 1937'
(1937), and, since it is also the traditional ballad form, John Keats's
'La Belle Dame Sans Merci' (1820);

Cinquain: the five-line stanza of Sir Philip Sidney's poems in *Astrophel
and Stella* (1591) (for example, 'Lover's Dialogue'), William Blake's
'Earth's Answer' (1794), Edwin Muir's 'The Combat' (1949);

Sixain: the six-line stanza of William Shakespeare's *Venus and Adonis*
(1593), Samuel Taylor Coleridge's *Rime of the Ancient Mariner*
(1798), Thom Gunn's 'Human Condition' (1957);

Seven-line stanza: Geoffrey Chaucer's *Troilus and Criseide* (1385) (*rime royal: ababbcc*); William Shakespeare's *The Rape of Lucrece* (1594), William Wordsworth's 'Resolution and Independence' (1807), Wilfred Owen's 'Insensibility' (1920);

Eight-line stanza: again, very common in English poetry, the form of Lord Byron's *Don Juan* (1819; *ottava rima: abababcc*) and *The Vision of Judgement* (1822), W. B. Yeats's 'Sailing to Byzantium' (1927), William Wordsworth's 'Solitary Reaper' (1807);

Nine-line stanza: (also known as the Spenserian stanza: the form of *The Faerie Queene* (1590–96)), in Lord Byron's 'Childe Harold's Pilgrimage' (1812–18), Percy Bysshe Shelley's 'Adonais' (1821), Philip Larkin's 'Church Going' (1955);

Ten-line stanza: as in John Keats's 'Ode on a Grecian Urn' (1820), and Percy Bysshe Shelley's 'The Revolt of Islam' (1818);

Eleven-line stanza: in John Keats's 'Ode to Autumn' (1820) and 'Ode to Psyche' (1820);

Twelve-line stanza: in Percy Bysshe Shelley's 'Hymn to Intellectual Beauty' (1817) and in W. B. Yeats's 'The Madness of King Goll' (1889).

Beyond the nine-line stanza (more or less the optimum stanza size in English poetry) the possibility of sustaining internal cross-references through sound, rhythm and meaning is much diminished, so that in Yeats's 'The Madness of King Goll', for example, the last line of each stanza is in fact a refrain repeated at the end of each group of lines. Similarly, in Richard Lovelace's (1618–58) 'Tom a Bedlam' the twelve-line stanza form is in fact an eight-line strophe with a four-line repeated refrain. Somewhere between nine and fourteen lines English poetry decides to look for methods of subdividing poetic shape, and at fourteen lines we have the shortest *complete* poetic genre, the sonnet, which Rossetti called 'a moment's monument'. Beyond fourteen lines English poetry is generally stichic in form. There is no *a priori* definition of the verse paragraph (but see Chapter 5, pp. 108–17 below).

The sonnet

There are two common forms of the fourteen-line sonnet: the *Petrarchan* (named after the Italian writer, Petrarch, 1304–74), which is divisible into an eight-line section (*octave*) and a six-line section (*sestet*) and has the rhyme-scheme *abbaabba cdecde*, first introduced into English poetry by Sir Thomas Wyatt (?1503–42) in the early sixteenth century and later used by Milton ('How soon hath Time') and William Wordsworth (1770–1850) ('Upon Westminster Bridge'); and the *English*, or *Shakespearean* sonnet, in which the rhyme scheme falls into three quatrains and a concluding couplet, *abab cdcd efef gg*. The concluding couplet clearly has the potential (and the attraction) of a summary and epigrammatic conclusion.

With a variation in the sestet, Wordsworth wrote a miniature history of practitioners of the Petrarchan sonnet form (English, Italian and, in the case of Camoens, Portuguese), but with a rather lame attempt to provide the 'twist' or 'turn' of the Shakespearean form's couplet:

Scorn not the Sonnet; Critic, you have frowned,	a
Mindless of its just honours; with this key	b
Shakspeare unlocked his heart; the melody	b
Of this small lute gave ease to Petrarch's wound;	a
A thousand times this pipe did Tasso sound;	a
With it Camöens soothed an exile's grief;	c
The Sonnet glittered a gay myrtle leaf	c
Amid the cypress with which Dante crowned	a
His visionary brow: a glow-worm lamp,	d
It cheered mild Spenser, called from Faery-land	e
To struggle through dark ways; and when a damp	d
Fell round the path of Milton, in his hand	e
The Thing became a trumpet; whence he blew	f
Soul-animating strains – alas, too few!	f

This toy-like sonnet indicates nothing of its potential for toughness, intensity, compression, and wit, nor of its sometimes electrifying tension between expansion and contraction. In the Wordsworth example there is no organic connection between the three quatrains and the argument, since the process of statement is merely a sequence of examples. Its thematic structure ($13\frac{1}{2}$ lines plus $\frac{1}{2}$) is at odds with its poetic shape, and to no effect. By contrast, Drayton's Sonnet 61 (the English or Shakespearean variant), for example, contains three quatrains which are strongly marked by stages in a thought process, by syntax and punctuation, and by two key words at the beginning of both the octave and the sestet ('Since . . . Now . . .'). Here, the formal precision of the sonnet's design perfectly matches its rhetorical purpose. Ostensibly celebrating the end of an affair in the first two quatrains, the final quatrain and couplet reinforce a shift in the poet's resolve. The real intention (and hope) of the poet is found in the verb tense of the last line:

Since there's no help, come let us kiss and part;	a
Nay, I have done, you get no more of me,	b
And I am glad, yea, glad with all my heart	a
That thus so cleanly I myself can free;	b
Shake hands forever, cancel all our vows,	c
And when we meet at any time again,	d
Be it not seen in either of our brows	c
That we one jot of former love retain.	d

Now at the last gasp of love's latest breath,	*e*
When, his pulse failing, passion speechless lies,	*f*
When faith is kneeling by his bed of death,	*e*
And innocence is closing up his eyes,	*f*
Now if thou wouldst, when all, have given him over,	*g*
From death to life though mightst him yet recover.	*g*

Schematically, there are three ways of looking at this poem's form: as 12 + 2 lines; as 8 + 6 lines; as 4 + 4 + 4 + 2 lines. The rhyme scheme shapes the poem's argument into three quatrains, the first two celebrating with increasing *resolve* the end of a relationship, the third insinuating an increasing *hesitation* to accept the end, and a couplet which marks a 'turn' in the sonnet's argument. The result is an *aesthetic* sense of 4+4+4+2. Yet *only* the couplet is out of line with the rest of the poem's resolve to have done with the affair, and this suggests a *thematic* outline of 12 + 2. In fact, the point at which the sonnet's argument begins to turn in on itself is line 9, so the *argumentative* form is 8 + 6.

The architectural quality of the sonnet is best indicated by a diagram. Our intuitive sense of the sonnet's form is based on a highly developed and, to some poets, an apparently stifling set of constraints.

English or *Shakespearean sonnet*

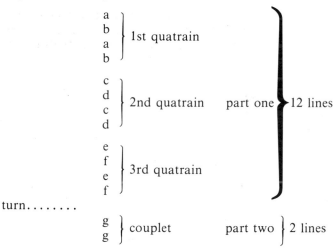

NOTE: the 'turn' in this English form is fairly heavily marked, since it needs to shift the tone or direction of the previous twelve lines. In Shakespeare's sonnets, turn 'markers' are *Then, If, Yet, Thus, So, And yet* and so on.

Petrarchan sonnet

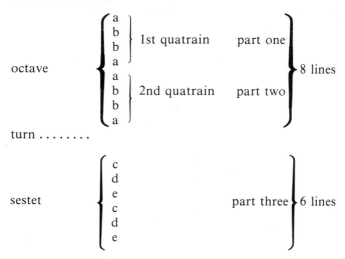

octave — 1st quatrain — part one
a
b
b
a

2nd quatrain — part two
a
a
b
b
a

} 8 lines

turn . . . .

sestet
c
d
e
c
d
e

part three } 6 lines

Spenserian variant of the English sonnet

This also has three quatrains and a final couplet, but overlaps the rhymes at the quatrain boundaries, in effect linking the quatrains by couplets. The result is an additional intensification of an already tightly organised structure, and an increase in musicality:

```
                a  }
                b  }  1st quatrain
                a  }
                b  }
couplet  {      b  }
                c  }  2nd quatrain
                b  }
couplet  {      c  }
                c  }
                d  }  3rd quatrain
                c  }
                d  }
                e  }  couplet
                e  }
```

NOTE: examples of this form will be found in Spenser's sonnet sequence *Amoretti* (1595).

Irregularity is an intrinsic part of metrical schemes, but the scope for variation within the sonnet form is very much more limited. Keats's 'On the Sonnet', for example, argues that efforts should be made to find more 'interwoven' rhyming schemes for the 'naked foot of poesy', in order to repair its 'pained loveliness'. The result is a rhyme scheme which defies all conventional patterns (*abcabdcabcdede*), and opinions will differ as to whether Keats has completely missed the point about the nature of the sonnet's intensely patterned idiom, or has in some way evolved a new form which reflects his radical plea for freedom. If we decide that the latter is true, then its success has little or nothing to do with the sonnet form. Like Wordsworth's sonnet quoted above (p. 43), Keats's poem is a perfectly acceptable 14-line poem which fails to exploit any of the sonnet form's 'sonnetness'. Without restriction there can be no freedom, and without pattern there is no innovation. The whole point about the sonnet form is that it provides the poet with a technical challenge to make fresh and his own that which may be inert and somebody else's, to give uniqueness to that which is conventional. In another context, and on the principle of metrical restraint versus metrical freedom, the critic J. V. Cunningham has this to say:

> Prose is written in sentences; poetry in sentences and lines. It is encoded not only in grammar, but also simultaneously in metre, for metre is the principle or set of principles, whatever they may be, that determine the line ... We have lost the repetitive harmony of the old tradition, and we have not established a new. We have written to vary or violate the old line, for regularity we feel is meaningless and irregularity meaningful. But a generation of poets, acting on the principles and practice of significant variation, have at last nothing to vary from.*

If, as has been said elsewhere, freedom is not a virtue in metre but only expressiveness, then the converse is also true, that is, that an elegantly disciplined form is successful only when it effectively and relevantly supports meaning. The Drayton sonnet above provides an expressive form for an argumentative process in a way that the Wordsworth example does not, and we might therefore say that Wordsworth has chosen not to exploit the intrinsic possibilities of the form. We might also conclude, however, that this choice leads to a bad poem! Sir Philip Sidney's sonnet, 'Loving in truth, and faine in verse my love to show' (the first in the sequence *Astrophel and Stella*, see pp. 24–5), actually confronts the problem of original use of conventional form and language as a subject. Its final couplet releases a sudden directness and simplicity after a tortuous and clotted octave. It *enacts* its subject whilst describing it; it *means* and *is* at the same time:

* Quoted in Paul Fussell, Jr., *Poetic Meter and Poetic Form*, Random House, New York, 1965, p. 163.

But words came halting forth, wanting Inventions stay,
Invention Natures child, fled step-dame Studies blowes,
And others feete still seem'd but strangers in my way.
Thus great with child to speake, and helpless in my throes
Biting my trewand pen, beating my selfe for spite,
Foole, said my Muse to me, looke in thy heart and write.

There is no 'given' connection between theme and poetic form.
Robert Herrick's 'The Pillar of Fame' (like Herbert's 'The Altar', see
pp. 13–14) provides a verbal shape for its central idea and, as the last
poem in Herrick's *Hesperides*, provides an ingenious and concrete image
of the idea that literary monuments can defeat the poet's enemy,
mortality:

Fame's pillar here at last we set,
Out-during marble, brass, or jet;
Charmed and enchanted so
As to withstand the blow
Of overthrow:
Nor shall the seas,
Or outrages
Of storms, o'erbear
What we uprear;
Tho' kingdoms fall,
This pillar never shall
Decline or waste at all;
But stand for ever by his own
Firm and well-fixed foundation.

To his book's end this last line he'd have placed:
Jocund his Muse was, but his life was chaste.

When Shakespeare turned to this theme he cast his thoughts into the
pre-existent sonnet form. The idea of earthly transience vanquished by
the permanence of art is the boast of sonnet XVIII, a beautiful example
of the idea that the sonnet can, by the successful fusion of content and
form, itself become a small eternity:

Shall I compare thee to a summer's day?
Thou art more lovely and more temperate:
Rough winds do shake the darling buds of May,
And summer's lease hath all too short a date:
Sometime too hot the eye of heaven shines
And often is his gold complexion dimmed;
And every fair from fair sometimes declines,
By chance or nature's changing course untrimmed;

But thy eternal summer shall not fade,
Nor lose possession of that fair thou ow'st;
Nor shall death brag thou wander'st in his shade,
When in eternal lines to time thou grow'st:
    So long as men can breathe, or eyes can see,
    So long lives this, and this gives life to thee.

The sheer naturalness and organic wholeness of this poem conceal the most consummate art. We can imagine no other way of expressing this poem's theme, though we may be aware that other *forms* do exist. (For further discussion and analysis of the sonnet form, see Chapter 5, pp. 85–9, below.)

Thematic form

Above the fourteen-line sonnet, notions of poetic form are dealt with not by line-groupings but by theme. In poetic kinds such as the aubade (or dawn poem), elegy, pastoral, ode, song, lyric, epic, and so on, nothing predetermines the stanza or strophic form. Until the end of the eighteenth century, however, classical forms retained a certain degree of formal identity and also required a certain appropriateness of language. Johnson's belief in the principle of linguistic decorum meant that to him Shakespeare had committed a disastrous error in using 'low' language in 'high' tragedy. Referring to Lady Macbeth's speech,

Come, thick Night!
And pall thee in the dunnest smoke of Hell,
That my keen knife see not the wound it makes;
Nor Heav'n peep through the Blanket of the dark,
To cry, hold, hold!

(Macbeth, I.5.34–8)

Johnson writes,

> while I am endeavouring to impress on my Reader the Energy of the Sentiment, I can scarce check my Risibility, when the Expression forces itself upon my Mind; for who can, without some Relaxation of his Gravity, hear of *Divinities peeping thro' a Blanket*.
>
> (The Rambler, No. 168, 1751)

That this was so suggests that Johnson's period had clearly demarcated literary forms and literary language into categories. Indeed, a hierarchy of poetic *kinds* was maintained, based on the practice of classical poets such as Virgil (70–19BC), proceeding from pastoral, georgic, didactic, elegiac, to the highest *kind* of all, that is epic. The list of these classical poetic forms, given below, might be described as the outline *curriculum vitae* for the careers of Spenser, Milton, Pope and Keats.

pastoral: a poem which ostensibly deals with rural life, originated by the Greek Theocritus, who wrote about Sicilian shepherds in the third century BC, and later imitated by Virgil. Other terms used are *idyll* (as in Theocritus's poems), *eclogue* (Virgil's title), and *bucolic poetry* (from the Greek word for 'herdsman');

ode: originally, short poems in lyric metres, but now the term covers lengthy lyric poems which are serious in subject, elevated in style, and with an elaborate stanzaic structure, as in the Greek odes of Pindar (*c.*522BC–*c.*440BC), with strophe, antistrophe, and epode;

georgic/didactic: as in Virgil's *Georgics* (*c.*37–30BC), 'agricultural poems', ostensibly about rural industry, but shading into instructive poetry, as in Pope's 'Windsor Forest', (1713), and *An Essay on Criticism,* (1711);

elegy: originally, in Greek and Roman poetry, any poem composed in a special elegiac metre, and in English any serious meditative poem, but the term is now generally used to describe *by theme* any poem concerned with the death of a particular person, or of man in general, as in Tennyson's 'In Memoriam' (on the death of his friend Arthur Hallam), or Shelley's *Adonais: An Elegy on the Death of John Keats,* or the 'Elegy Written in a Country Churchyard' (1750) by Thomas Gray (1716–71);

heroic/epic: as in the *Iliad* and *Odyssey* by Homer (*c.*ninth century BC), in the anonymous *Beowulf* (of which the manuscript dates from the late tenth century AD) and in *Paradise Lost,* a lengthy narrative poem which combines the fate of individuals with that of a race, tribe, or nation. The Greek philosopher Aristotle (384–322BC) placed *tragedy* at the top of this hierarchy of genres, above epic, but later critics and commentators reversed the preference. The intellectual and artistic requirements of epic are vast. Keats attempted an epic twice, but left both attempts unfinished. Milton devoted years of his life to *Paradise Lost,* 'to justify the ways of God to man'. An alternative to original epic is translation of the original, as in Pope's translation of the *Iliad* and *Odyssey* ('ten years to comment and translate', as Pope put it). Additionally, the epic provoked various types of satirical variants, both in verse and prose, as in Dryden's *Mac Flecknoe* (1682), Pope's *The Rape of the Lock* (1714: a comic epic), Pope's *The Dunciad* (1728, 1742: a mock-epic), Henry Fielding's (1707–54) *Joseph Andrews* (1742: 'a comic epic poem in prose' – Author's Preface).

The table on p. 50 indicates a continuity of these forms in outline, although it does not include equally important forms such as the *epistle* (which evolves from Horace and is used by Pope and Keats, for example), or the *ode* (stretching from Ovid (43BC–AD18), through the 'Horatian Ode Upon Cromwell's Return from Ireland' (1681) by Andrew Marvell (1621–78), to the odes of Abraham Cowley (1618–87),

THE CONTINUITY OF FORMS

Pastoral/Eclogue	Georgic/Didactic	Elegiac	Heroic/Epic/Tragedy
Theocritus, *Idylls* (3rd century BC)	Hesiod, *Works and Days*		Homer, *Iliad*, 24 books; *Odyssey*, 24 books
Virgil, *Eclogues* (c.42–47BC)	*Georgics*, 4 books (c.37–30BC)	Ovid (43BC to AD18), *Elegies*	Virgil, *Aeneid*, 12 books (c.30–19BC)
Sir Philip Sidney, *Arcadia* (1590: a pastoral romance)			George Chapman, translation of *Iliad* (1611) and *Odyssey* (1614–15)
Edmund Spenser, *The Shepheards Calendar* (1579); *A Pastoral Aeglogue on the Death of Sir Philip Sidney*		*The Teares of the Muses; The Ruines of Rome*	*The Faerie Queene*, 7 books (1590–1609)
John Milton, 'Arcades' (?1633)		*Lycidas* (1637: a pastoral elegy)	*Paradise Lost*, 12 books (1667); *Paradise Regained*, 4 books (1671); *Samson Agonistes* (1671: 'a dramatic poem')
Alexander Pope, *Pastorals* (1709); *Messiah: A Sacred Eclogue* (1712)	'Windsor Forest' (1713); *An Essay on Criticism* (1711); *An Essay on Man* (1734)	'Elegy to the Memory of an Unfortunate Lady' (1717)	'Eloisa to Abelard' (1717); two choruses to the tragedy of *Brutus* (fragments of an epic); *The Rape of the Lock* (1714) and *The Dunciad* (1728–43) – both 'mock-epic' in form; translation of *Iliad* (1720), *Odyssey* (1726)
John Keats, 'I stood tip-toe upon a little hill' (1817)			*Hyperion*, 3 books (1820: unfinished); *The Fall of Hyperion* (a dream vision: unfinished: 1818)
Percy Bysshe Shelley		*Adonais* (1821)	*The Cenci* (tragedy: 1819); *Prometheus Unbound* (1820)
W. H. Auden		'At the Grave of Henry James' (1941)	
Louis MacNeice, 'An Eclogue for Christmas' (1949)			

to Thomas Gray's ode 'The Progress of Poesy' (1757), William Wordsworth's 'Ode: Intimations of Immortality' (1807) and the odes of Keats (1820)). Again, the point to bear in mind is not rigid categorisation, but the fluidity of all these genres. In the odes of Shelley and Wordsworth, for example, the title *ode* may tell us something about the tone and language of the poem in advance, but nothing about its shape on the page, since by this point in English literary history the neo-classical idea of pre-existent or 'public' forms had lost its cogency. Poets also combine or merge different forms, a notable example being the pastoral elegy. They also, of course, invent new forms for new voices.

Essentially, there are two concepts of poetic form: that forms pre-exist in past models, and that form is *organic* to the particular and individual poetic experience and to no other. In the first sort, there is the advantage of a recognisable genre and a determined language of expression, as in the pastoral and sonnet; in the second, the apparent freedom to determine form from within. But when we apply this general paradigm to specific examples we may find that the theory operates only as a guide-line, and not as an axiom. Wordsworth's sonnet 'Upon Westminster Bridge, September 3, 1802' is an inherited form given an intensely particularised and intimate significance related to a specific moment in his poetic autobiography. Equally, there is a vast distance between, say, Milton's use of the pastoral elegy as a *metaphor* in *Lycidas* and Wordsworth's *Michael: A Pastoral Poem*, where 'the humble and rustic life' is not a metaphor but the actuality of financial ruin, the hard economics of agricultural tenure, the destruction of family ties. Wordsworth writes *against* rather than *inside* our literary preconceptions of the pastoral genre. Without our conventional expectations that April is a commonplace focus for poetic celebrations of love and the re-birth of natural life in the spring, the ironic opening of T. S. Eliot's *The Waste Land* would fail to convey its full anti-romantic disillusion ('April is the cruellest month, breeding/Lilacs out of the dead land . . .').

The use of a pre-existing form is a type of allusion (see Chapter 4, section on 'Allusion', pp. 68–74 below, for a fuller discussion), and may depend for part of its effect on our awareness of an implied comparison between the model and the specific example. In its extreme form, parody, a model is actually imitated in order to attack it, as in Sir John Squire's parody* of Gray's 'Elegy'. The fourth and fifth stanzas of Gray's poem are:

> Beneath those rugged elms, that yew tree's shade,
>   Where heaves the turf in many a moldering heap,
> Each in his narrow cell forever laid,
>   The rude forefathers of the hamlet sleep.

* For Squire's parody in full, see Arnold Silcock, ed., *Verse and Worse*, Faber & Faber, London, 1952, pp. 90–3.

The breezy call of incense-breathing Morn,
　The swallow twittering from the straw-built shed,
The cock's shrill clarion, or the echoing horn,
　No more shall rouse them from their lowly bed.

Squire's version (stanzas two and three) is:

Here where the flattering and mendacious swarm
　Of lying epitaphs their secrets keep,
At last incapable of further harm
　The lewd forefathers of the village sleep.

The earliest drug of half-awakened morn,
　Cocaine or hashish, strychnine; poppy-seeds
Or fiery produce of fermented corn
　No more shall start them on the day's misdeeds.

This is close, textual parody. The one exists as a parasite on the other, replacing a sombre meditation by cynical worldliness, amusing because of its nervous proximity to something we take seriously. This example juxtaposes form and content, exploding the one by the other. Additional relationships are illustrated by Marlowe's 'Passionate Shepherd to his Love', which elicited a reply from Sir Walter Raleigh (c.1552–1618) in 'The Nymph's Reply to the Shepherd', and from Donne, in 'The Baite'. Within the general form of pastoral dialogue, each poem uses an identical metrical shape (iambic tetrameter quatrains, rhyming *aabb*), and their inter-relationship establishes a miniature genre. Marlowe's poem begins, 'Come live with me and be my love'; Raleigh's poem begins,

If all the world and love were young,
And truth in every shepherd's tongue,
These pretty pleasures might me move
To live with thee and be thy love

(clearly responding to Marlowe's romantic idealism with a dose of hard-headed realism), and Donne's poem ('Come live with mee, and bee my love') gently parodies the whole idea of being caught in love's snares. The formal relationship extends here to a *thematic continuity*: each poem implicitly and explicitly builds on the others.* A relationship *without* formal signposts but through ideas is illustrated in the short poem 'Merciles Beaute' by Geoffrey Chaucer. Here, Chaucer mischievously

---

* The tradition continues. See C. Day Lewis's poem (from *The Magic Mountain*, 1933), first stanza:

Come live with me and be my love,
And we will all the pleasures prove
Of peace and plenty, bed and board,
That chance employment may afford.

plays with the conventional symptoms of courtly love, such as the 'killing' eyes of a pitiless mistress, the misery of a lover condemned to worship at a distance, and so on. In the third and final section, one of the conventions (that the true lover languishes and grows thin) is neatly turned on its head:

Sin I fro Love escaped am so fat,
I never thenk to ben in his prison lene;
Sin I am free, I count him not a bene.

The lover's plumpness and health indicate that he lacks the true lover's symptoms: therefore he cannot have been in love at all. An effect in the convention becomes a cause of its denial.

When a form or a convention becomes stiff in the joints, outmoded or dead to all new usage, it may still provide a useful disguise for the unexpected. Poems about a mistress's eyes run the risk of banality, but the Restoration poet and wit Charles Sackville, Earl of Dorset (1638–1706) employed this overworked topic deliberately. He begins with a formula, qualifies it, and ends with a violent twist of conventional expectations:

Dorinda's sparkling wit and eyes
    United cast too fierce a light,
Which blazes high, but quickly dies,
    Pains not the heart, but hurts the sight.

Love is a calmer, gentler joy,
    Smooth are his looks, and soft his pace,
Her Cupid is a blackguard boy,
    That runs his link full in your face.

A more brutal opposition between a whole series of hackneyed poetic images of (romanticised) female beauty and their physical roots is found in Donne's 'The Comparison'. It is as though the poet's ability to 'compose' an image of beauty in words can just as skilfully be deconstructed (or even de-composed) by the facts of human ugliness:

Like Proserpine's white beauty-keeping chest,
Or Jove's best fortunes urne, is her fair brest.
Thine's like worme eaten trunkes, cloth'd in seal's skin
Or grave, that's dust without, and stinke within.   (lines 23–6)

In this example, the conventional expectations and their antidote alternate line by line in an internal debate, although Donne's range of imagery is characteristically vast.

The classic statement of the relationship between the individual poet and the context of past poets is T. S. Eliot's essay 'Tradition and the Individual Talent':

No poet, no artist of any art, has his complete meaning alone. His significance, his appreciation is the appreciation of his relation to the dead poets and artists. You cannot value him alone; you must set him, for contrast and comparison, among the dead. I mean this as a principle of aesthetic, not merely historical, criticism. The necessity that he shall conform, that he shall cohere, is not one-sided; what happens when a new work of art is created is something that happens simultaneously to all the works of art which preceded it. The existing monuments form an ideal order among themselves which is modified by the introduction of the new (the really new) work of art among them.*

The only way this 'contrast and comparison' can be achieved by the reader, of course, is by knowing a great number (theoretically, all) of the poems ever printed. However, we have noted in this section the ways in which poems signal links through *generic* similarities, which operate on a 'whole poem' level; how conventional or inherited ideas set up expectations which are confirmed or qualified within an individual poem (sometimes by a simple title); and the way in which poetic forms as such may evolve. When Dr Johnson read Gray's 'Elegy' he noticed how it 'abounds with images which find a mirror in every mind, and with sentiments to which every bosom returns an echo' (*Life of Gray*). Now although Johnson praises this poem for its universality, or its truth-to-life, and hence for its human insight, it is also possible that Johnson meant something quite specific about its construction by using the phrase 'to which every bosom returns an echo'. Certainly, Gray's 'Elegy' is one of the most densely allusive elegies ever written, unusually dependent not only for its form but also for its phrasing and individual words on previous pastoral elegies. Its dependency is not overtly signalled, but the literary memory is triggered constantly. For example, Gray's line 17,

The breezy call of incense-breathing Morn

evokes Milton's lines 193–4 in Book IX of *Paradise Lost*,

the humid flowers that breath'd
Their morning incense

* This essay was first published in 1919, and later collected in *The Sacred Wood: Essays on Poetry and Criticism*, Faber & Faber, London, 1920. Its influence has been enormous, which perhaps explains the virulence of Philip Larkin's counterblast in *Poets of the 1950s* (1955):

As a guiding principle I believe that every poem must be its own sole freshly-created universe, and therefore have no belief in 'tradition' or a common myth-kitty or casual allusions in poems to other poems or poets, which last I find unpleasantly like the talk of literary understrappers letting you see that they know the right people. A poet's only guide is his own judgment . . .

This textual allusiveness, if concentrated and sustained, provides a sense of inevitability, 'recognisability', and echo, from a reader already sensitive to the genre. Reading a poem like the 'Elegy' is like looking in a mirror which reflects literary and not visual objects. It is to this subject of literary signs that we must turn in the next chapter. But first, we might examine Eliot's observation on tradition and the individual talent in relation to one of the genres mentioned above, the pastoral.

The pastoral

To some extent, the value of exploiting a traditional form or idea is that a poet may infer as well as state meanings. Pastorals had been written by Virgil in Latin, Theocritus in Greek, and Spenser (among many others) in English before Milton wrote his *Lycidas*. Assuming such an awareness in his reader, Milton inherits and deploys certain conventional relationships between himself and his reader, and between himself and his subject: that he and his student friend Edward King (1612–37), whose drowning in the Irish Sea was the occasion for Milton's elegy, were both 'shepherds' (a metaphor which includes fellow-poets, fellow-scholars, and co-religionists). One of the 'new' inflections which Milton provides in this classical (hence pagan) form is the Christian metaphor of the shepherd as pastor of spiritual sheep. The conventional pattern evolves new uses in Milton's hands. If it does not, that is, if the conventional machinery of the form is retained with its bearings seized up, then its only use is as a literary fossil. This is what happens in *The Shepherd's Week* (1714) by the poet John Gay (1685–1732). Here, the sophisticated metaphor of the pastoral becomes a literary in-joke and is used to evoke an urban man's condescension directed at rustic idiocy:

CUDDY: Hold, witless *Lobbin Clout*, I thee advise,
Lest blisters sore on thy own tongue arise.
Lo Yonder *Cloddipole*, the blithesome swain,
The wisest lout of all the neighbouring plain!
From *Cloddipole* we learnt to read the skies,
To know when hail will fall, or winds arise.
He taught us erst the heifer's tail to view,
When stuck aloft, that show'rs would strait ensue;
He first that useful secret did explain,
That pricking corns foretold the gath'ring rain.

In the third section of *The Waste Land*, Eliot also evokes the pastoral convention, but this time for a new purpose, and signals the (ironic) juxtaposition between the old and the new by an allusion to Spenser's marriage song *Prothalamion*. Eliot writes:

The river's tent is broken: the last fingers of leaf
Clutch and sink into the wet bank. The wind
Crosses the brown land, unheard. The nymphs are departed.
Sweet Thames run softly till I end my song.
The river bears no empty bottles, sandwich papers,
Silk handkerchiefs, cardboard boxes, cigarette ends
Or other testimony of summer nights. The nymphs are departed.

In a poem characterised by mechanical and loveless relationships the evocation of Spenser's pastoral poetry *infers* the comparative squalor of contemporary sexual relationships and *infers* an historical decline in human values. Eliot triggers a broad reference to Spenser's poem by quoting its single-line refrain:

Then forth they all out of their baskets drew
Great store of Flowers, the honour of the field,
That to the sense did fragrant odours yield
All which upon those goodly Birds they threw,
And all the waves did strew,
That like old *Peneus* Waters they did seeme,
When down along by pleasant *Tempes* shore,
Scattred with Flowres, through *Thessaly* they streeme,
That they appeare, through Lillies plenteous store,
Like a Brydes Chamber flore.
Two of those *Nymphes*, meane while, two Garlands bound,
Of freshest Flowres which in that Mead they found,
The which presenting all in trim Array,
Their snowie Foreheads therewithall they crownd,
Whil'st one did sing this Lay,
Prepar'd against that Day,
Against their Brydale day, which was not long:
    Sweete *Themmes!* runne softly, till I end my Song.

The immediately noticeable property of Eliot's allusion is its economy: in a few words it evokes a great deal of Spenser. It has meaning, of course, only if the reader is able to hear the echo, and the fact that Eliot felt it necessary to mark this reference to Spenser in a footnote suggests that the modern reader has lost much of the necessary conditioned literary response Eliot requires. Loss of a vital poetic tradition is one of the crucial differences between a society which cherishes literary continuities and one which does not. In the Spenser passage the same requirements are made of the contemporary Elizabethan reader: Spenser draws parallels between the river that flows through London and the Peneus, the principal river in Thessaly which flows between Mount Olympus (the seat of the Greek gods) and Mount

Ossa. Eliot uses more direct signals of cultural decline, however, as in that traditional symbol of spontaneous lyrical song, the nightingale. To modern, 'dirty' ears, it sounds like this:

Twit twit twit
Jug jug jug jug jug jug

and there is the self-explanatory cultural travesty of the lines in the pub music

O O O O that Shakespeherian Rag –
It's so elegant
So intelligent

The pastoral has always been a dissatisfied townsman's vision of a better life, exchanging the imperfect man-made city for the unspoilt and God-given country. At least since classical times, it has evoked a Golden Age perfection enjoyed before the fall of Adam and his expulsion from the garden of Eden.* Dean Swift's (1667–1745) innocuously titled poem 'A Description of the Morning' (1704: text given in Chapter 5, p. 81 below) is in fact an urbanised georgic, replacing the machinery of a rural dawn poem with the setting, sights and sounds of a dawn in town. A careful reader will see that although only one word ('Flock') signals the pastoral transformations directly, its last line suggests the powerful theme of the death of innocence. Having described the petty deceits and the less petty corruptions of the city, Swift concludes:

And School-Boys lag with Satchels in their Hands.

Between this line and Virgilian pastoral stands Shakespeare's pastoral comedy *As You Like It*. Jaques's famous speech on the seven ages of man includes the lines:

And then the whining school-boy, with his satchel,
And shining morning face, creeping like snail
Unwillingly to School.   (II.7.145–7)

The innocence of youth and the idealism of pastoral are soon to be submerged in the moral decline of age and the city.

* For further brief discussion, see Peter V. Marinelli, *Pastoral*, Methuen, London and New York, 1971.

Chapter 4

Language

Poetry is the only mode of written communication in which it is
normal for all the words to mean what they say.
> (Hugh Kenner, *The Art of Poetry* (1959))

For want of a nail the shoe was lost,
For want of a shoe the horse was lost,
For want of a horse, the rider was lost,
For want of a rider, the kingdom was lost –
> (William Golding, *The Spire* (1964), quoted from
> Benjamin Franklin's *Poor Richard's Almanack* (1758))

To see a World in a Grain of Sand
And a Heaven in a Wild Flower,
Hold Infinity in the palm of your hand
And Eternity in an hour.

A Robin Red breast in a Cage
Puts all Heaven in a Rage.
A dove house fill'd with doves & Pigeons
Shudders Hell thro' all its regions.
A dog starv'd at his Master's Gate
Predicts the ruin of the State.
A Horse misus'd upon the Road
Calls to Heaven for Human Blood.
Each outcry from the hunted Hare
A fibre from the brain does tear.

A skylark wounded in the wing,
A Cherubim does cease to sing.
> (William Blake, 'Auguries of Innocence' (1803))

Metaphor, simile and symbol

A road-sign is a symbol, an intrinsically meaningless sign endowed with
a highly specialised meaning by its context. Its significance is clear only
to those who know already the context in which it is to be understood,
say, a bend in the road. It is efficient because it functions without verbal
language. It is a diagram in space which represents a physical

phenomenon. In poetry, a symbol is a sign which stands for or signifies something else, or something more than its literal self. This *transfer of meaning* is commonly marked by a *simile*, as in 'The World' (1650) by Henry Vaughan (1622–95):

> I saw Eternity the other night,
> Like a great *Ring* of pure and endless light,

where the transfer is signalled by the word 'like' (or 'as'). The most extensive transfer of meaning, into a completely parallel mode of expression, is *allegory* (as in Spenser's *The Faerie Queene*, or George Orwell's (1903–50) prose satire *Animal Farm* (1945)), where there are no overt signals of transferred meaning but a consistent pattern of cross-references (to the education of a gentleman in Spenser, and to communism in Orwell). Between these two types of *local* and *extensive* transfers of meaning there is *metaphor* and *symbol*.

Simile transfers its meaning overtly, metaphor covertly, but both have two parts: a *tenor* and a *vehicle* (terms invented by I. A. Richards in his *Philosophy of Rhetoric*, 1936). The tenor of Burns's simile 'O my love's like a red, red rose' is 'my love', since this is its principal subject; the vehicle, or secondary subject, is 'red, red rose'. What actually happens when tenor and vehicle are employed is that the combination of two things produces a third – X is like Y in respect of Z. The third thing shares *some* of the characteristics of the other two, but not others. For example, in *Spectator*, 62 (1711) Joseph Addison (1672–1719) showed how the comparison between a mistress's bosom and the whiteness of snow could be neatly destroyed by adding the comment that it was as cold too. For effective use a metaphor and a simile must point to resemblances. Metaphoric statement can 'say' things for which there is no verbal form: it produces a two-way link and a double focus.

Transfers of meaning and types of metaphor

conceit: an elaborate and striking parallel established between two dissimilar things, as in the example from Henry Vaughan above. The *metaphysical conceit* as used by John Donne and his followers was described by Johnson as 'a kind of *discordia concors*, a combination of dissimilar images, or discovery of occult resemblances in things apparently unlike'. In 'A Valediction Forbidding Mourning' Donne compares the spiritual unity and physical separation of himself and his lady with a pair of compasses:

> If they be two, they are two so
>   As stiff twin compasses are two;
> Thy soul, the fixed foot, makes no show
>   To move, but doth if the other do.

synecdoche: a part which represents a whole, as in Gray's polite reference to a buried corpse in the 'Elegy':

> Here rests his *head* upon the lap of Earth
> A youth to Fortune and to Fame unknown

and in the reference to painting and music in the second line of Yeats's 'Lapis Lazuli':

> I have heard that hysterical women say
> They are sick of *the palette and fiddle-bow.*

metonymy: the name of one thing applied to another with which it is closely associated: 'I have been reading Swift' instead of 'the books by Swift'. Metonymy actually describes all types of metaphoric transference, but it tends to sharpen the commonplace and vague (if not say anything new).

personification: an inanimate or abstract thing endowed with human attributes or feelings, as in Hamlet's soliloquy in Shakespeare's *Hamlet* II.2.601–2

> For murder, though it have no tongue, will speak
> With most miraculous organ . . .

and in a poem of 1650 by James Shirley (1596–1666):

> Devouring Famine, Plague, and War,
>   Each unable to undo Mankind
> Death's servile emissaries are

John Ruskin (1819–1900), the art critic and social reformer, invented the term 'pathetic fallacy' (1856) in order to expose the morbidity of this type of personification as an emotional indulgence. It now survives without this derogatory sense.

compound metaphor: the merging of two levels of metaphoric transfer, as in the fourth line of Hamlet's speech in *Hamlet*, III. 1.56–9:

> To be, or not to be: that is the question:
> Whether 'tis nobler in the mind to suffer
> The slings and arrows of outrageous fortune,
> Or to take arms against a sea of troubles,
> And by opposing end them.

This example of compound metaphor looks odd: a sword is not much use for repelling the sea. It is in fact a brilliantly precise image of Hamlet's melodramatic futility. It might be compared with Milton's reference to the clergy in *Lycidas*

> Blind mouthes! That scarce themselves know how to hold
> A sheep-hook.

Even if, as has been suggested, we think of the 'blind mouth' as being a tapeworm inside a sheep's carcase, the transfer from shepherds/pastors to shepherd's crook/bishop's crozier, and then to both of the latter held in the mouths of each of the former (though blind), we are confused by the concentration of transfers. This seems to qualify as a 'mixed metaphor', an inelegance of style. It should be distinguished from 'compound metaphor' by its confusion.

dead metaphor: one transfer in which there is, literally, no life, as in 'the arm of a chair', where the transfer has passed into common usage and no longer directs our attention to the referred meaning. Its poetic use is seen in Swift's 'A Love Song. In the Modern Taste' (1733):

> Mild *Arcadians*, ever blooming,
>   Nightly nodding o'er your Flocks,
> See my weary Days consuming,
>   All beneath yon flow'ry Rocks

where the whole (extended) pastoral metaphor of lovers-as-shepherds is exploded by absurdly overdone transfers ('*ever* blooming' and 'Nightly nodding'). If the pastoral represents a state of mind, Swift implies, here is a state of utter mental vacuity.

extended metaphor: as the term implies, a metaphor which is developed through a number of related transfers of meaning. The octave of Donne's fifth sonnet is an extended metaphor:

> I am a little world made cunningly
> Of Elements, and an Angelike spright,
> But black sinne hath betraid to endless night
> My worlds both parts, and (oh) both parts must die.
> You which beyond that heaven which was most high
> Have found new sphears, and of new lands can write,
> Powre new seas in mine eyes, that so I might
> Drowne my world with my weeping earnestly,
> Or wash it, if it must be drown'd no more.   (lines 1–9)

allegory: the ultimate extension of metaphor, where one thing is described almost entirely and at length in terms of another. Allegory bears the same relationship to symbol as extended metaphor does to a single metaphor. Spenser's *The Faerie Queene* is an allegory, an 'Allegorie, or darke conceit', whose purpose was 'to fashion a gentleman or noble person in vertuous and gentle discipline ... coloured with an historicall fiction' (author's preface). Its *tenor* or principal subject is therefore twelve moral virtues, its vehicle the history of King Arthur and his court. The Redcrosse Knight in Book I is St George, the patron saint of England, who also represents the virtue of Holiness, as Sir Guyon in Book II represents Temperance.

These are the most familiar types of transferring meaning by comparison. Frequently, *inferred metaphors* will be found, as in Pope's line 'And ten low words oft creep in one dull line' (*Essay on Criticism*), where the word 'creep' allied to the rhythmic quality suggests that a (suppressed) animal or reptilian image is being used, and again in Pope's satirical portrait of Sporus, 'Wit that can creep, and Pride that licks the dust' (*Epistle to Dr. Arbuthnot*).

The difference between a metaphor and a symbol is best illustrated by specific examples, but in doing this it is useful to recognise two very broad categories of symbolic language, public and private.

Public and private imagery

A Christian reader of *Paradise Lost* would expect that many of his religious beliefs would find confirmation in this poem: a Muslim reader might be surprised at the number of parallelisms with his own faith, but would nevertheless read the poem as the manifestation of a different spiritual culture external to his own concerns. Every poet battles with the prospect of losing his individual voice in a common language and attempts to shape public language to his own needs. Eliot's phrase 'April is the cruellest month' has an altogether unintended meaning for someone who lives in the tropics, where it may be a fact and not a literary irony that humans retreat before the 'dead season' of scorching heat. If Milton uses the public narrative of the Christian creation myth, he can nevertheless give it an intensely private meaning. The test of an image's success is not whether it has been used before (as in a *convention*), but *how expressive* it is for the particular purpose. Poetry which stays inside a convention may be nothing more than inert conventional writing, but as in the use of a given metrical scheme, the challenge to manipulate what is already there into something new and original may be irresistibly exciting. Equally, other poets have evolved original and private systems which replace conventional patterns completely. This may be illustrated by comparing Chaucer's use of an image with Blake's use of the same image. Chaucer uses the rose and the garden as images in *The Romance of the Rose*, keyed to some known significances in medieval romance as a genre: for instance the description of Beauty, led in by the God of Love, lines 1013–16:

> Hir fleshe was tendre as dew of flour;
> Hir chere was symple as byrde in bour;
> As whyt as lylye or rose in rys,
> Hir face gentyl and tretys.

Blake uses the rose as an image in a very brief poem entitled 'The Sick Rose':

O Rose, thou art sick!
The invisible worm
That flies in the night,
In the howling storm,

Has found out thy bed
Of crimson joy,
And his dark secret love
Does thy life destroy.

Both poets are concerned with love as a theme (tenor), and both poets use a metaphoric mode (vehicle) to express it. Chaucer signals the transfer of meaning by three overt comparisons and an implied one, Blake more covertly by imagining a human and passionate (though sinister) relationship between worm and rose. Chaucer is talking *implicitly* about the psychology of love, in which the rosebud is the symbol of female sexual acceptance, Blake is talking *explicitly* about a rose, whilst hinting at the human experience of love which is destroyed by an unstated antagonist (in which case the worm may represent jealousy, or envy, or suspicion). Chaucer uses a series of similes in an overall context of allegory, Blake uses a single image as a symbol. Chaucer's rose is part of a whole grammar of inter-related images given specific meaning by conventional or generic use: the French poets Guillaume de Lorris and Jean de Meun had used it in the same way before Chaucer. Blake's image requires no external reference for its meaning. Yet both poems are read with a double focus. In each case the reader's response is enriched and deepened if we know that the rose may be associated with love, beauty and transience. Shelley's 'To a Skylark' (1820) has a rose which is deflowered by the wind at the moment of its full bloom; in Yeats's 'The Rose of the World' (1892), it is used as an image of transience, and again in 'The Secret Rose' (1896). The frequency of its use indicates not only the conventionality of the image but also its evolution of *different* meanings. Yeats, for example, remarked of 'The Rose of the World': 'I notice upon reading these poems for the first time for several years that the quality symbolized as The Rose differs from the Intellectual Beauty of Shelley and of Spenser in that I have imagined it as suffering with man and not as something pursued and seen from afar.'*

In practice then, a clear distinction between the use of private imagery (*variation*) and public imagery (*convention*) does exist but is difficult to sustain, since the one contributes to the other.

Doubtless, some one individual poet must have been the first to perceive the symbolic potential of the rose. But the language of poetic

---

* W. B. Yeats's own note (1925). See P. Allt and R. K. Alspach, eds., *Variorum Edition of the Poems of W. B. Yeats*, Macmillan, New York, 1903, p. 842.

symbol, like language itself, grows both by anonymous contributions and by identifiable 'strong' individual usage, each of which is taken into the common stock of expressive resources. A symbol is a kind of metaphor, but its reference (or *tenor*) may be both rich *and* indeterminate. Unlike the road-sign, it denotes not a single meaning but a complex of possible meanings other than and in addition to those of its literal self. What we must accept is that a symbol may be the *only* means of a poet's expression. What we cannot accept is poetry in which symbol or metaphor is a *substitute* for meaning, as for example in the forced and elaborate opening stanza of Richard Crashaw's (1612–49), *The Weeper* (1648):

> Haile, Sister Springs,
> Parents of Silver-footed rills!
> Ever bubling things!
> Thawing Crystall! Snowy Hills!
> Still spending, never spent; I meane
> Thy faire eyes, sweet *Magdalen.*

Thirty-one stanzas on Mary Magdalen's tears (described at one point as 'Two walking Baths, two weeping motions;/Portable and compendious Oceans') is poetic overkill. But Blake's 'The Tyger' (1794) scintillates with a highly charged and felt energy of thought and expression, simply expressed but awesome in its *range* of symbolic mystery:

> Tyger! Tyger! burning bright
> In the forests of the night:
> What immortal hand or eye
> Could frame thy fearful symmetry?
>
> In what distant deeps or skies
> Burnt the fire of thine eyes?
> On what wings dare he aspire?
> What the hand dare seize the fire?   (lines 1–8)

No poet before or after Blake has seen the tiger as a symbol of the beauty and terror of divine creation, but then few poets share Blake's *habitual* perception of the world through its minute and particular parts, each inter-related in a cosmic whole:

> The Harlot's cry from Street to Street
> Shall weave Old England's winding Sheet.
> The Winner's Shout, the Loser's Curse,
> Dance before dead England's Hearse.
>
> Every Night & every Morn
> Some to Misery are Born.

Every Morn & Every Night
Some are Born to sweet delight.
Some are Born to sweet delight,
Some are Born to Endless Night.

('Auguries of Innocence', lines 115–24)

Whereas the example from Crashaw above shows a poet ransacking Nature for increasingly elaborate images, Blake's method shows an extraordinary precision of reference to commonplace (or at least intelligible) objects which are then transformed by their symbolic weight. 'Silver-footed rills' as an analogy for the descent of tears on a cheek is not inherently ridiculous, but its use suggests that Crashaw's poetic imagination is not focused on anything but *words*. Blake's symbols are simultaneously *seen* for what they are and for what they stand for; however complex the latter may be it remains inseparable from the former because Blake's symbol is not just a literary device but a way of seeing.

The following list of examples indicates in very broad outline the distinction between poetry which serves a public purpose through the use of public themes, purposes, and language (imagery in particular) and poetry which evolves a relatively private or alternative language and focus.

THE WORLD	THE POET
Public or conventional theme and image	*Private theme and image*
Biblical narratives: as in Milton's *Paradise Lost* (the Creation myth in epic form) or in *Samson Agonistes* (form of Greek tragedy re-cast, Samson being the Israelite hero (Book of Judges)).	The complex symbolism of Blake's 'Universal Man' and the 'Four Mighty Ones'; a complete mythology of his own creation, *The Four Zoas, Jerusalem,* and *Milton.*
Greek mythology, as in the use by Shelley ('The World's Great Age'), and Donne ('The Autumnall') of the Greek notion of the first period of mankind as a 'Golden Age'.	Robert Graves's 'the white Goddess', a depiction of the female principle of inspiration in 'The White Goddess'. The Nigerian poet, Wole Soyinka, adopts the tribal god Ogun as his own artistic patron, in *Idanre* (1967).
The poet in society	*The poet outside society*
The poet as shepherd (a convention stemming from Virgil and Theocritus and exemplified in Spenser, Milton and Shelley); the poet as the public voice (Dryden's poems to Cromwell, Charles II, and Pope's 'Windsor Forest'); client to patron.	The poet as social outcast, as in Cowper's 'The Castaway'; as spiritual misfit, in Thomas Hardy's 'The Impercipient (At a Cathedral Service)', or as an abandoned seer (Arnold's 'Dover Beach'); the poet as social critic: Pope's *Dunciad.*

THE WORLD (cont.)	THE POET (cont.)
Public voices	*Private voices*
For example, the 'bardic' poetry of Old English (e.g. *Beowulf*); Gray's 'The Bard', and 'The Progress of Poesy' (which uses the Aeolian lyre as an oracular voice); didactic poetry, such as Pope's *Essay on Man*; most satire.	The image of the lyre or harp of Aeolus, played by the wind, and used as a symbol of intimately personal poetry and as an image of artistic creativity: as in the last stanza of Shelley's 'Ode to the West Wind', Coleridge's 'The Aeolian Harp', 'Dejection: An Ode', and in Keats's 'To my brother George'.
Poetry using contemporary intellectual or scientific ideas: Shakespeare's 'Tudor myth' in the history plays; Donne's use of alchemical and cosmological ideas.	Yeats's language of symbols, elaborated in his book *A Vision* (1925), and used throughout his poetry starting with 'The Magi' – the use of Celtic myth and legend, imagery of winding stairs, spirals, and gyres, as in 'The Second Coming', where the gyre is a figure for dissolutionary change in a cycle of history. Cf. also 'Under Ben Bulben'.

All poetry which is circulated, either in manuscript or in printed or in oral form, is a public statement. Imagery which similarly circulates among a community of poets becomes a common resource. The most public role of poetry is as epic, usually drawing its subject from the great events of history (as in the fall of Troy and the subsequent adventures of Aeneas, from whom all the Roman emperors claimed descent, in Virgil's *Aeneid*), or biblical myth (as in Milton's version of the Fall of Man in *Paradise Lost*), or national history (as in Pope's projected epic on the eponymous founder of Britain, *Brutus*). The poet's role in epic poetry, and therefore his language and imagery, is dominated by a public function. Thus Dr Johnson describes the subject of Milton's epic as of universal significance, not merely

> the destruction of a city, the conduct of a colony, or the foundations of an empire. His subject is the fate of worlds, the revolutions of Heaven and Earth; rebellion against the supreme King, raised by the highest order of created beings; the overthrow of their host, and the punishment of their crime; the creation of a new race of reasonable creatures; their original happiness and innocence, their forfeiture of immortality, and their restoration to hope and peace ... Before the greatness displayed in Milton's poem, all other greatness shrinks away. The weakest of his agents are the highest and noblest of human beings, the original parents of mankind; with whose actions the elements consented; on whose rectitude, or deviation of will, depended the state of human nature, and the condition of all the future inhabitants of the globe.

Milton's opening lines are general, alluding to facts already known to a community of Christian believers, who are also assumed able to hear the syntactic link back to the opening lines of the *Aeneid* ('Arma virumque cano': Of arms and the man I sing):

Of man's first disobedience, and the fruit
Of that forbidden tree whose mortal taste
Brought death into the world, and all our woe,
With loss of Eden, till one greater Man
Restore us, and regain the blissful seat,
Sing, Heavenly Muse . . .

As early as line six, Milton has substituted Virgil's own voice ('I sing') for a 'private' variation: the Muse here is not the classical and pagan Urania, muse of epic poetry, but the Holy Spirit of the Bible which inspired Moses to write Genesis.

Few poets in English since Milton have attempted the epic. It has come to be synonymous with length, but far more significantly, its requirement for the poet to speak on behalf of civilisation itself can no longer be met, neither can its assumptions about its audience be taken for granted. Even so, vast historical significance, if combined with highly particularised images as allusions, can still be possible. The obvious example is T. S. Eliot's *The Waste Land*, but consider the three stanzas of Yeats's 'Long-legged Fly' (1939):

That civilisation may not sink,
Its great battle lost,
Quiet the dog, tether the pony
To a distant post;
Our master Caesar is in the tent
Where the maps are spread,
His eyes are fixed upon nothing,
A hand under his head.
Like a long-legged fly upon the stream
His mind moves upon silence.

That the topless towers be burnt
And men recall that face,
Move most gently if move you must
In this lonely place.
She thinks, part woman, three parts a child,
That nobody looks; her feet
Practise a tinker shuffle
Picked up on a street.
Like a long-legged fly upon the stream
Her mind moves upon silence.

That girls at puberty may find
The first Adam in their thought,
Shut the door of the Pope's chapel,
Keep those children out.
There on that scaffolding reclines
Michael Angelo.
With no more sound than the mice make
His hand moves to and fro.
Like a long-legged fly upon the stream
His mind moves upon silence.

Yeats has caught three heroic figures in an intensely private moment: Caesar, an emperor who will dominate the known world; Helen of Troy, over whom dynasties will clash; Michelangelo, at work on the Sistine chapel ceiling, whose art will strike posterity as superhuman in its excellence. Their *known* significance in human history is juxtaposed with an *unconscious* moment in their individual lives: a world turns on such insignificant moments of vacancy, as fleeting and as precarious as an insect floating on the process of time itself.

Allusion

In the poem by Yeats above, there are two types of reference pointing us beyond the poem. The first is to history (Roman, for Caesar; Greek, for Helen of Troy; Renaissance art history for Michelangelo; Christian myth for Adam). The second stanza signals the identity of 'she' by a second functionally different reference, a literary allusion. Yeats's line about the 'topless towers' evokes the lines in Marlowe's *Doctor Faustus* (1604, 1616):

Was this the face that launched a thousand ships
And burnt the topless towers of Ilium?
Sweet Helen, make me immortal with a kiss.   (V.1.98–100)

Yeats is making a claim on our literary awareness by using a kind of literary shorthand. The reference, or allusion, is signalled by a literal quotation whose function is to bring to mind a controlled association of two contexts. Yeats does not evoke the whole of Marlowe's tragedy by doing this, only the legendary magnificence of Helen's beauty and the cause of the Trojan wars. Yet it is an intensely suggestive phrase. The fact that we recognise it as an allusion contributes to the pleasure of the poem, and enables us to add to Yeats's context. The same intensification of meaning arises if we recall that Shakespeare also had borrowed Marlowe's lines for *Troilus and Cressida* (II.2.81), 'why, she is a pearl,/Whose price hath launch'd above a thousand ships'. In both examples the borrowed material is incorporated into its new context without interruption or pause, and without specific indication of the indebtedness.

A definite signal of borrowing may be the use of an epigraph, as when Eliot prefaces *The Waste Land* with a quotation from Dante's *Inferno*, and again *The Hollow Men* with a quotation from *Heart of Darkness* (1902) by the novelist Joseph Conrad (1857–1924), or by the use of a marked quotation. Apart from these devices, there is no way of establishing, or proving, whether an allusion is either conscious or unconscious. The crucial question is its effect. When Milton's Satan says, 'Which way I fly is hell, myself am hell', the question is not about the fact of the borrowing but its effect on meaning. Marlowe's Mephistopheles had said, 'Why this is hell, nor am I out of it' (*Doctor Faustus*, I.3.77).

Conflating the fallen Angel, Satan, with the degraded Mephistopheles clearly broadens, deepens, and sharpens Milton's line. It may also mean that we respond to *both* texts thereafter in the light of each other. This kind of allusion indicates how a skilled poet can possess and re-use existent material. Only an inept poet will *depend* for his effects on the work of others. Pope attacks the bad dramatists of his day in *The Dunciad* for this kind of perverse dependency, otherwise known as plagiarism:

> Here to her chosen all her works she shows;
> Prose swelled to verse, verse loit'ring into prose:
> How random thoughts now meaning chance to find,
> Now leave all memory of sense behind . . .
> How, with less reading than makes felons scape,
> Less human genius than God gives an ape,
> Small thanks to France, and none to Rome or Greece,
> A past vamp'd future, old, revived, new piece,
> 'Twixt Plautus, Fletcher, Shakespeare, and Corneille,
> Can make a Cibber, Tibbald, or Ozell.
>
> (Book I, lines 273–6; 281–6)

This whole passage itself begins as a parody of Christ's temptation by Satan.

As Pope indicates, allusion which depletes the original in order to enrich the derived text is nothing short of theft. An allusion enriches by evoking additional and appropriate meanings and, as one commentator puts it, 'the best borrowers are those who have abundance of their own; the great capitalists who, having large possessions, can make use of their loans from others.'* This is how Johnson argued against the charge that literary quotation is a form of pedantry, in an age when the centrality of literature to the idea of culture was undoubted:

* E. E. Kellett, *Literary Quotation and Allusion*, Heffer, Cambridge, 1933, p. 43.

'No, Sir, it is a good thing; there is a community of mind in it. Classical quotation is the *parole* of literary men all over the world.' To which Wilkes replied, 'Upon the continent they all quote the vulgate Bible. Shakespeare is chiefly quoted here; and we quote also Pope, Prior, Butler, Waller, and sometimes Cowley.'*

The twentieth-century poet and reader dare not assume such a community of mind, however. If allusions work only on readers who already know the source of the allusion, then this suggests that it can only work in the context of a shared culture. If the poet is aware of its disintegration he may, as Yeats did, evolve his own mythological framework of references, or, as Philip Larkin has done, dispense with *literary* allusion altogether, or, as Eliot did, signal the literary allusions by adding explanations in footnotes. No serious reader of poetry can be ignorant for long of the possibility of one poet holding some form of dialogue with his predecessors. And yet there *is* a problem for the modern poet in search of an audience but uncertain of an assumed cultural identity. Whereas Johnson's 'The Vanity of Human Wishes' (1749) could uphold Christian fortitude as the answer to the question

> Must helpless Man, in Ignorance sedate,
> Swim darkling down the current of his Fate?

the closing lines of 'Dover Beach' (*c.*1851) by Matthew Arnold (1822–88), provide no such public consolation:

> . . . we are here as on a darkling plain
> Swept with confused alarms of struggle and flight,
> Where ignorant armies clash by night.

W. B. Yeats declares this sense of disintegration in 'The Second Coming' (1921):

> Things fall apart; the centre cannot hold;
> Mere anarchy is loosed upon the world

and in 'Three Movements' he fixes on lost *literary* continuities precisely:

> Shakespearean fish swam the sea, far away from land;
> Romantic fish swam in nets coming to the hand;
> What are all those fish that lie gasping on the strand?

This conviction of a breakdown in spiritual and literary continuities is, paradoxically, a *structural* principle in Eliot's *The Waste Land*: each borrowing is a fragment 'shored against my ruins', as Eliot said, and it is through allusion that Eliot constructs an image of what has been lost.

In order of explicitness, we might list the types of borrowing thus:

* Boswell's *Life of Johnson* (1791), entry for 8 May 1781.

(1) *Acknowledged or marked quotations:* as in the first five lines of Eliot's 'Journey of the Magi':

> 'A cold coming we had of it,
> Just the worst time of the year
> For such a journey, and such a long journey:
> The ways deep and the weather sharp,
> The very dead of winter.'

Here the marked quotation (also acknowledged in Eliot's *Notes*) is adopted almost verbatim from a Nativity sermon by the seventeenth-century divine Lancelot Andrewes, and serves as a starting point for a meditation on the spiritual, political and physical discomfort of the Magi. A further example of the marked quotation is Eliot's use, signalled by italics and the original language, of Dante's *Purgatorio* in *The Waste Land*.

(2) *Unmarked borrowings:* as in the Marlowe–Shakespeare–Yeats example above concerned with Helen of Troy. This is the broadest class of *allusion*, in which the *adopted* text is assumed to be known to the reader and which therefore contributes to the *adopting* text's meaning. For example, Eliot's 'A Game of Chess' episode in *The Waste Land* begins with the lines:

> The Chair she sat in, like a burnished throne,
> Glowed on the marble, where the glass
> Held up by standards wrought with fruited vines
> From which a golden Cupidon peeped out

which calls to mind Enobarbus's description of the first meeting between Antony and Cleopatra in Shakespeare's play *Antony and Cleopatra* (II.2.195 and ff.):

> The barge she sat in, like a burnish'd throne,
> Burn'd on the water; the poop was beaten gold,
> Purple the sails, and so perfum'd, that
> The winds were love-sick with them . . .

Eliot's lady is no Cleopatra, and the allusion functions ironically, that is, not to enrich but to impoverish, by activating two texts simultaneously, the first associated with a magnificent passion, the second with suffocating and sterile sensuousness. The quotation from Shakespeare is signalled by specific and literal quotation.

(3) *Echo:* in the above example we might also detect an additional but unmarked remembrance of the opening lines of Milton's *Paradise Lost*, Book II, and the description of Satan:

High on a Throne of royal state, which far
Outshone the wealth of Ormus and of Ind,
Or where the gorgeous East with richest hand
Showers on her kings barbaric pearl and Gold,
Satan exalted sat . . .

But here there are no literal verbal similarities. Though there may be a thematic and situational parallel with Eliot's lines, the earlier text is not activated as part of the latter's textual meaning. It can only be described as an echo. In passing, however, we might observe how these lines evolve as *allusion* in Dryden's *Mac Flecknoe* (lines 106–7):

The hoary prince in majesty appeared,
High on a throne of his own labours reared

and again in Pope's *Dunciad* (1743: Book II, lines 1–5):

High on a gorgeous seat, that far outshone
Henley's gilt tub, or Fleckno's Irish throne,
Or that where on her Curls the public pours,
All-bounteous, fragrant grains and golden showers,
Great Cibber sate . . .

Pope alludes to Dryden, but fleshes out his portrait from the Miltonic original.

(4) *Parallelism:* often a shared context or pattern of imagery, but not requiring cross-reference, as in parallels of theme and image between *Nosce Teipsum* (1599), by Sir John Davies (1569–1626):

Much like a subtile spider, which doth sit
In middle of her web, which spreadeth wide;
If aught do touch the utmost thread of it,
She feels it instantly on every side

and Pope's couplet in *An Essay on Man* (1734):

The spider's touch, how exquisitely fine!
Feels at each thread, and lives along the line.

(5) *Concealed borrowings:* of various kinds, including plagiarism, and not necessarily or very frequently designed to fool the reader; but sometimes capable of a startling effect, as when Swift allows one of his defenders in *Verses on the Death of Dr. Swift* (1731) to praise Swift's originality by silently stealing a line from the elegy on Abraham Cowley by Sir John Denham (1615–69):

To steal a Hint was never known,
But what he writ was all his own.

A more important category is represented by Gray's 'Elegy', where large numbers of unmarked borrowings, echoes and parallelisms are silently incorporated in a new way.* An extreme form of this technique is the *cento*, a poem which is entirely constructed from other poems. The following example, slightly re-punctuated, has been constructed from Eliot's *The Waste Land*, Byron's *Don Juan*, Wordsworth's *Michael*, Blake's 'Nurse's Song', Arnold's *Thyrsis*, Yeats's 'The Circus Animals' Desertion', Tennyson's 'Tithonus', 'An English Summer' (1963) by Elizabeth Jennings (*b*.1926), and 'Do not Go Gentle into that Good Night' by Dylan Thomas (1914–53):

> Under the brown fog of a winter dawn
> That isle is now all desolate and bare.
> Near the tumultuous brook of Greenhead Ghyll,
> The days of my youth rise fresh in my mind.
>
> Runs it not here, the track by Childsworth Farm?
> Heart-mysteries there, and yet when all is said,
> The woods decay, the woods decay and fall.
> Rage, rage against the dying of the light.

Identifying a literary allusion (of whatever kind) is one thing; evaluating its effect is another. No one who has read, say, Eliot's own notes at the end of *The Waste Land* can be left in doubt that a poet may have all sorts of reasons, or none in particular, for literary allusion. 'I am not familiar with the exact constitution of the Tarot pack of cards, from which I have obviously departed to suit my own convenience,' Eliot warns his readers in the first part of *The Waste Land*. Equally, Yeats comments on his poem 'Among School Children', 'I have taken the "honey of generation" from Porphyry's essay on "The Cave of the Nymphs", but find no warrant in Porphyry for considering it the "drug" that destroys the "recollection" of pre-natal freedom. He blamed a cup of oblivion given in the zodiacal sign of Cancer.' A poet writes with his own warrant. Of 'The Tower', title poem in *The Tower* (1928), Yeats feels drawn to admit, 'In the passage about the Swan in Part III I have unconsciously echoed one of the loveliest lyrics of our time – Mr. Sturge Moore's "Dying Swan".' Many a poet's lines owe their immortality to their use by a later and greater talent which has possessed them and turned them to greater account. In such cases the usual sense of indebtedness backwards in time is reversed, for the standards of literary excellence are uncompromising. A poet's intentions are always interesting, but hardly definitive. D. H. Lawrence warned the reader to

---

* For a commentary on the 'Elegy' and its allusiveness, see Roger Lonsdale, ed., *The Poems of Thomas Gray, William Collins, Oliver Goldsmith*, Longman, London, 1971, pp. 109, 117–41.

trust the tale, not the teller, and T. S. Eliot (perhaps somewhat disingenuously) is said to have remarked on a discrepancy between private and public meaning in *The Waste Land*:

> Various critics have done me the honour to interpret the poem in terms of criticism of the contemporary world, have considered it, indeed, as an important bit of social criticism. To me it was only the relief of a personal and wholly insignificant grouse against life; it is just a piece of rhythmical grumbling.*

* See Valerie Eliot, ed., *The Waste Land: A Facsimile and Transcript of the Original Drafts*, Faber & Faber, London, 1971, p. 1.

Readings of poems

IN THIS SECTION a number of poems have been chosen for detailed scrutiny. It is not an attempt in any sense to 'cover' the vast range of English poetry, nor to suggest that the poems chosen are in some way 'touchstones' of their type. A poem is typical only of itself, although it inevitably shares some of its characteristics with other poems. The reader who has struggled this far, however, will rightly expect to find out how the material in Part One can usefully be applied to specific examples. To someone coming to a serious study of poetry for the first time there will seem to be a frustrating lack of certainties in the task of interpretation. Prosodic analysis may provide ascertainable 'facts' about metre, structure, shape, and so on, but no matter how significant these may be, the task of *evaluating* a poem includes and goes beyond formal analysis. Like Graham Greene's whisky priest, readers discover that poetry can be dangerous.

Each of the following sections contains at least two poems, since the task of criticism is at root a matter of comparing and contrasting. The poems are related in terms of either a shared theme or form, but different in their period, treatment, tone, style, or purpose.

Narrative

John Keats, 'La Belle Dame Sans Merci' (1820)

O what can ail thee, Knight at arms,
    Alone and palely loitering?
The sedge has withered from the Lake
    And no birds sing!

O what can ail thee, Knight at arms,   5
    So haggard, and so woebegone?
The squirrel's granary is full
    And the harvest's done.

I see a lily on thy brow
    With anguish moist and fever dew,   10
And on thy cheeks a fading rose
    Fast withereth too.

I met a Lady in the Meads,
   Full beautiful, a faery's child,
Her hair was long, her foot was light   15
   And her eyes were wild.

I made a Garland for her head,
   And bracelets too, and fragrant Zone;
She looked at me as she did love
   And made sweet moan.   20

I set her on my pacing steed
   And nothing else saw all day long,
For sidelong would she bend and sing
   A faery's song.

She found me roots of relish sweet,   25
   And honey wild, and manna dew,
And sure in language strange she said
   "I love thee true."

She took me to her elfin grot
   And there she wept and sighed full sore,   30
And there I shut her wild wild eyes
   With kisses four.

And there she lulléd me asleep,
   And there I dreamed, Ah Woe betide!
The latest dream I ever dreamt   35
   On the cold hill side.

I saw pale Kings, and Princes too,
   Pale warriors, death-pale were they all;
They cried, "La belle dame sans merci
   Thee hath in thrall!"   40

I saw their starved lips in the gloam
   With horrid warning gapéd wide,
And I awoke, and found me here
   On the cold hill's side.

And this is why I sojourn here,   45
   Alone and palely loitering;
Though the sedge is withered from the Lake
   And no birds sing.

From Samuel Taylor Coleridge's *The Rime of the Ancient Mariner* (1798)

PART II

The Sun now rose upon the right:
Out of the sea came he,
Still hid in mist, and on the left
Went down into the sea.

And the good south wind still blew behind,   5
But no sweet bird did follow,
Nor any day for food or play
Came to the mariner's hollo!

And I had done a hellish thing,
And it would work 'em woe: 10
For all averred, I had killed the bird
That made the breeze to blow.
Ah wretch! said they, the bird to slay,
That made the breeze to blow!

Nor dim nor red, like God's own head,   15
The glorious Sun uprist:
Then all averred, I had killed the bird
That brought the fog and mist.
'Twas right, said they, such birds to slay,
That bring the fog and mist.   20

The fair breeze blew, the white foam flew,
The furrow followed free;
We were the first that ever burst
Into that silent sea.

Down dropped the breeze, the sails dropped down, 25
'Twas sad as sad could be;
And we did speak only to break
The silence of the sea!

All in a hot and copper sky,
The bloody Sun, at noon   30
Right up above the mast did stand,
No bigger than the Moon.

Day after day, day after day,
We stuck, nor breath nor motion;
As idle as a painted ship   35
Upon a painted ocean.

Water, water, everywhere,
And all the boards did shrink;
Water, water, everywhere,
Nor any drop to drink.   40

The very deep did rot: O Christ!
That ever this should be!
Yea, slimy things did crawl with legs
Upon the slimy sea.

About, about, in reel and rout   45
The death-fires danced at night;
The water, like a witch's oils,
Burnt green, and blue and white.

And some in dreams assuréd were
Of the Spirit that plagued us so;   50
Nine fathoms deep he had followed us
From the land of mist and snow.

And every tongue, through utter drought,
Was withered at the root;
We could not speak, no more than if   55
We had been choked with soot.

Ah! well-a-day! what evil looks
Had I from old and young!
Instead of the cross, the Albatross
About my neck was hung.   60

Probably the best-known *literary* ballad in English literature, Keats's poem re-creates both the form and some of the techniques and qualities of an ancient narrative genre rooted in *oral* poetry. Coleridge intended to write 'in imitation of the *style* as well as the spirit of the elder poets' ('Advertisement' to first edition of *Lyrical Ballads*, 1798), but his use of archaisms co-exists awkwardly with certain features such as overt symbolism, introspective analysis, and a very un-ballad like didacticism in lines 614–17:

He prayeth best, who loveth best
All things both great and small;
For the dear God who loveth us,
He made and loveth all.

Here are the opening stanzas of the border ballad 'Sir Patrick Spens', collected and printed by Thomas Percy (1721–1811) in *Reliques of Ancient English Poetry* (1765), but probably composed 300 years earlier:

> The king sits in Dunfermline toune,
> Drinking the blude-reid wine:
> O quhar will I get a guid sailor,
> To sail this schip of mine?
>
> Up and spak an eldern knicht,
> Sat at the kings richt kne:
> Sir Patrick Spence is the best sailor,
> That sails upon the se.

Keats uses a similar stanza form, but with two significant variations from this traditional form. 'Sir Patrick Spens' alternates a four-stress iambic line with a three-stress iambic line, rhyming *abcb*: Keats's stanza has three consecutive iambic tetrameters contracting to a two-stress final line, but also rhyming *abcb*. Each form provides a *minimal* but completely regular rhyme-scheme within a *maximally* regular metrical form. In both examples we have regular clarity of *shape* allied to a mysteriousness of plot. In Keats there is another structural pattern, the repetition of lines or phrases (lines 1 and 5, 2 and 46, 3 – 4 and 47 – 8), which suggest a circularity in the poem's movement.

The traditional ballad has a story to tell, but no doubt due to its evolution as an oral form, the contents of the narrative are reduced to events rather than explanations of events. Keats preserves this mysteriousness, whereas Coleridge interpolates a structure of symbols (in the last two lines of Part II the Albatross symbolises the Mariner's guilt and replaces the crucifix, symbol of salvation). The form of the Keats poem is a dialogue: a question from an unidentified speaker occupies the first three stanzas and the remaining nine seem to provide an answer. There is no response to that answer from the narrator, but introductory imagery provides indicators of his anxiety and sense of deep foreboding (the lily, associated with death, and the fading rose with a dying love). Natural imagery, then, provides a powerfully *suggestive* introduction and context. Coleridge's poem is also a dialogue, for the Mariner's punishment is to tell his guilt to anyone who will listen, to expurgate his crime against God's Nature.

Nature in Keats's poem is inhospitable and silent witness to the knight's tragic tale of loss and despair. He attempts to recapture a dream-like relationship with a fatally attractive and pitiless woman. It is a love mingled with exquisite pain and death; though the final stanza resists explanation, its mystery underlies the central fascination of the poem's theme. The love of a mortal man for a supernatural woman, and the unbridgeable gap between them, provides a yearning for unity where there is no hope of reunion, a pursuit of unachievable bliss. The poem implies that the reunion is only possible through death, but until then the knight is left with a precious vision, tortured by pain and love.

Keats's extraordinary skilfulness in fusing mystery of theme with unobtrusively evocative language contrasts not only with Coleridge's more self-conscious text (the use of medievalisms such as 'Eftsoons' and 'merry minstrelsy', and also the addition of marginal explanations in prose), but with Wordsworth's brief narrative in ballad-form 'Lucy Gray; or, Solitude' (1799), where artful simplicity of form and mysteriousness of meaning both drop into the trite and even (unintentional) ludicrousness:

They followed from the snowy bank
Those footmarks, one by one,
Into the middle of the plank;
And further there were none!   (lines 53–6)

This is information; there is nothing for the reader to do but accept it. But when Keats cuts his last line to half its expected length, we are left with both a metrical vacancy and a sense of spiritual loss simultaneously:

Though the sedge is withered from the Lake
    And no birds sing

It is as though Nature herself has died. Moreover, the implications which lie between the two extremes of *manna* and *thrall* in lines 26 and 40 are vast: the first, a food divinely provided, hence used in the Eucharist, and the second, with its tones of satanic possession. To be strung between these extremes is the knight's sentence, and for the reader it provides a moment of simultaneous intellectual and emotional growth.

'La Belle Dame Sans Merci' was written in April 1819, and should be read alongside 'The Eve of St. Agnes' (January–February 1819). For further examples of the ballad and narrative forms, see A. E. Housman, *A Shropshire Lad* (1896); Oscar Wilde, *Ballad of Reading Gaol* (1898); Hugh MacDiarmid, *A Drunk Man Looks at the Thistle* (1926); W. H. Auden's 'Miss Gee' (1937), the first stanza of which is

Let me tell you a story
    About Miss Edith Gee;
She lived in Clevedon Terrace
    At number 83.

The following provide further examples of the genre: James Kinsley, ed., *The Oxford Book of Ballads*, Oxford, 1969; Matthew Hodgart, ed., *The Faber Book of Ballads*, Faber & Faber, London, 1965; and Anne Ehrenpreis, ed., *The Literary Ballad*, Arnold, London, 1966.

Subject and treatment

Jonathan Swift, 'A Description of the Morning' (1709)

Now hardly here and there an Hackney-Coach
Appearing, showed the Ruddy Morn's Approach.
Now Betty from her Master's Bed had flown,
And softly stole to discompose her own.
The Slipshod Prentice from his Master's Door   5
Had par'd the Dirt and sprinkled round the Floor.
Now Moll had whirled her Mop with dext'rous Airs,
Prepared to Scrub the Entry and the Stairs.
The Youth with Broomy Stumps began to trace
The Kennel-Edge, where Wheels had worn the Place.   10
The Smallcoal-man was heard with Cadence deep,
'Till drowned in Shriller Notes of Chimney-Sweep.
Duns at his Lordship's Gate began to meet,
And Brickdust *Moll* had scream'd through half the Street.
The Turnkey now his Flock returning sees,   15
Duly let out a-Nights to steal for Fees.
The watchful Bailiffs take their silent Stands,
And Schoolboys lag with Satchels in their Hands.

William Wordsworth 'Upon Westminster Bridge, Sept. 3, 1802'

Earth has not anything to show more fair:
    Dull would he be of soul who could pass by
    A sight so touching in its majesty:
This City now doth, like a garment, wear
The beauty of the morning; silent, bare,   5
    Ships, towers, domes, theatres, and temples lie
    Open unto the fields, and to the sky;
All bright and glittering in the smokeless air.
Never did sun more beautifully steep
    In his first splendour, valley, rock, or hill;   10
Ne'er saw I, never felt, a calm so deep!
    The river glideth at his own sweet will:
Dear God! the very houses seem asleep;
    And all that mighty heart is lying still!

Both of these poems are concerned with morning in the city, but within
the thematic genre of *aubade* each indicates some of the contrasting
qualities of 'Augustan' and 'Romantic'. The dominant tone and subject
of poetry in the first half of the eighteenth century is urban. Jonathan

Swift, Matthew Prior (1664–1721), Pope and Johnson write about man in society, not man set against the natural world of physical nature. It was Dr Johnson who said, 'He who is tired of London is tired of life.' Occasionally, however, the Augustan poet's fondness for adapting classical forms runs against his urban-centred world, as when Johnson must recommend the virtues of rural retreat *from* the city's corruption in *London* because he is imitating (in 1738) the third satire of the great Roman satirist Juvenal (*c.*65–130AD). This contrasts markedly with his antagonism towards the artificiality of Milton's pastoral elegy *Lycidas*, whose insincere fiction he found 'easy, vulgar, and therefore disgusting'. Wordsworth, on the other hand, found London in 1791 a 'monstrous anthill on the plain' (*The Prelude*, Book VII, 149), and his radical distaste for the corrupting effect of the city on the human personality is expressed everywhere. But in this poem he seems overawed by its uncharacteristic (and unexpected) beauty.

Swift's title implies that this is a typical morning in the city, and he clearly sees its subject from street level. It is, however, much more than a 'description'. Wordsworth is standing at some distance from the city, and his title implies that the experience described is highly specific, rather like a diary entry of some autobiographical significance. Swift's poem tells us nothing about the physical appearance of the city, but is full of human activity. Wordsworth's city shows no sign of human life, and is seen as an inert body at rest.

The tone of each poem is the key to its meaning. Moral judgments are to be *inferred* in the first poem (nobody is actually working at their assigned task, most are concerned merely to give the appearance of occupation), and there is at least one example of overtly criminal activity (the gaoler in line 15 who releases his prisoners at night to steal). All may seem to be description, but the tone of irony suggests moral censure. A sequence is implied in the last line in an otherwise incrementally shaped poem, since it is the younger generation who stand as fascinated witnesses to their elders' deceits. Swift has glimpsed the 'real' nature of the city before its ugliness has been camouflaged by day. The final line also contributes to a sub-textual strategy, since it evokes Jaques's speech in Shakespeare's pastoral comedy *As You Like It* (II.7.145–7):

And then the whining school boy, with his satchel,
And shining morning face, creeping like snail
Unwillingly to school.

If this reference is picked up by the reader it will hint at the underlying pastoral paradigm, which is specifically indicated only once in the text (by 'Flock' in line 15). These two references signal an ironic twist in a poem which has almost completely transformed the conventional pastoral dawn poem into its seedy urban equivalent. Beauty is exchanged for squalor, innocence for corruption, oneness with nature for human struggle against a sordid environment. The dawn is signalled not by bird-song but by the creaking of a hackney coach and a cacophony of street-cries. Pastoral love has been translated into casual and covert immorality (lines 3–4), and the shepherd of the pastoral has become a corrupt official of the law. Form and content are thus played off against the shadow of a familiar but indirectly stated convention for the purpose of satire. The 'voice' of the satirist is therefore the public censor. Charles Cotton's 'Morning Quatrains' (1689), by contrast, is more bluntly satirical than Swift's poem. Cotton includes shepherds and milk-maids, but also lines such as this:

And manufacturers of each trade
By op'ning shops are open laid,

and his schoolboys are accompanied by a moral confession:

The slick-fac'd schoolboy satchel takes,
And with slow pace small riddance makes;
For why, the haste we make, you know,
To knowledge and to virtue's slow.   (lines 51–2, 65–8)

Swift's poem is therefore written against a background and a genre which it is assumed the reader will already know. By contrast, Wordsworth's poem requires no previous literary awareness. Its use of the sonnet form is a matter largely of tone rather than structure, and in spite of its apparent specificity in line 6 it is not concerned with looking at the city but rather with the effect the city has on the spectator himself. Its mood is one of surprised exaltation, its theme one of unaccustomed beauty in a normally despised object. Also drawn, like Swift, to compare the urban with the rural dawn, Wordsworth concludes that they are equally beautiful and pacific. If there is a division in the poem, it is a residual 'turn' between lines 8 and 9 (corresponding to the octave–sestet division), but the structural unity of this poem is maintained by the uniformly ecstatic tone and language, including the use of exclamatory punctuation in lines 11 and 14. It clearly lacks the epigrammatic 'turn' of the Shakespearean sonnet form in its last couplet, as if to underline the fact that there is no 'argument' here, but in its place a climactic moment of joy.

In spite of their very different functions, both poems employ the iambic pentameter line, and performance of each poem will indicate that the line tends towards four rather than five stresses. Swift's poem is built up from heavily end-stopped couplets. The only exception to this is the first line, with its breathless aspirants, which announces in sound the ugliness of content to come. Each couplet is a complete sentence, and most of the poem's characters occupy a couplet each. The effect is that of a portrait constructed of separate and specific details. The necessary *frame* for the details is the inferred pastoral background. Wordsworth's sonnet (*abba acca dedede*) is metrically far more flexible, and after the first three lines the highly mobile caesura and run-on lines create a sense of mood shaping form. Nothing appears to stand in the way of its passionate progress.

The contrast between the country and the city in these two poems acquired an overt social and ethical significance in the 1780s, which Wordsworth himself exploited in *Michael: A Pastoral Poem*. In *The Village* (1783) by George Crabbe (1754–1832) the *literary* image of pastoral is starkly juxtaposed with its realistic rural counterpart in eighteenth-century England. The result is a cutting social irony:

> Fled are those times, when, in harmonious strains,
> The rustic poet praised his native plains:
> No shepherds now, in smooth, alternate verse,
> Their country's beauty or their nymphs' rehearse;
> Yet still for these we frame the tender strain,
> Still in our lays fond Corydons complain,
> And shepherds' boys their amorous pains reveal,
> The only pains, alas! they never feel!
>
> On Mincio's banks, in Caesar's bounteous reign,
> If Tityrus found the Golden Age again,
> Must sleepy bards the flattering dream prolong,
> Mechanic echoes of the Mantuan song?
> From Truth and Nature shall we widely stray,
> Where Virgil, not where Fancy, leads the way?
>
> (Book I, lines 7–20)

The machinery of the Virgilian pastoral (as in the *Eclogues*) is now not only redundant but actually conceals the degradation of contemporary agricultural labour. The swains have departed because of land-enclosure and poverty, leaving only a literary echo, 'tinsel trappings of poetic pride'. Similarly, in *The Task* (1785) by William Cowper (1731–1800), where 'God made the country, and man made the town' (Book I, line 749), the idea of art transforming the ugly into the beautiful is exposed as a cheat. One hard look at the city will reveal that

> Thither flow
> As to a common and most noisome sew'r,
> The dregs and feculence of ev'ry land.
> In cities foul example on most minds
> Begets its likeness. Rank abundance breeds
> In gross and pamper'd cities sloth and lust,
> And wantonness and gluttonous excess.

In cities vice is hidden with most ease,
Or seen with least reproach; and virtue, taug
By frequent lapse, can hope no triumph ther
Beyond th'achievement of successful flight.
I do confess them nurs'ries of the arts,
In which they flourish most; where, in the beams
Of warm encouragement, and in the eye
Of public note, they reach their perfect size.
Such London is, by taste and wealth proclaim'd
The fairest capital of all the world,
By riot and incontinence the worst.

(Book I, lines 682–99)

Johnson's 'London' (1738) is still able to hold out the country as a past golden age, a conventional mental and moral restorative, but Blake's 'London' sees the city as the centre of bleak, horrific despair from which there is no escape:

But most thro' midnight streets I hear
How the youthful Harlot's curse
Blasts the new born Infant's tear
And blights with plagues the Marriage hearse.

Here, unlike Swift's poem, there is no game of literary allusion.

For further discussion, see Chapter 3, pp. 55–7 above. Eliot's juxtaposition of city and country follows conventional judgments. Thom Gunn's poem 'In Praise of Cities' (*The Sense of Movement*, 1957) does not. Its last line celebrates the city as 'Extreme, material, and the work of man'. Raymond Williams, *The Country and the City*, Chatto & Windus, London, 1973, relates literary pastoral to social contexts. Maynard Mack's *The Garden and the City: Retirement and Politics in the Later Poetry of Pope, 1731–1743*, Oxford University Press, 1969, treats the classical background of this idea in relation to Pope's poetry. Philip Larkin's poem 'Here' (*The Whitsun Weddings*, 1964) indicates the ironic potential of the pastoral form in its lines 'a terminate and fishy-smelling/Pastoral of ships up streets'.

Form and variation

William Shakespeare, Sonnet LX (*c.*1595)

Like as the waves make towards the pebbled shore,
So do our minutes hasten to their end,
Each changing place with that which goes before,
In sequent toil all forwards do contend.

tivity once in the main of light   5
Crawls to maturity, wherewith being crown'd,
Crooked eclipses 'gainst his glory fight,
And time that gave, doth now his gift confound.
Time doth transfix the flourish set on youth,
And delves the parallels in beauty's brow,   10
Feeds on the rarities of nature's truth,
And nothing stands but for his scythe to mow.
   And yet to times in hope my verse shall stand
   Praising thy worth, despite his cruel hand.

John Donne, 'Holy Sonnet' VI (published 1633)

This is my playes last scene, here heavens appoint
My pilgrimages last mile; and my race
Idly, yet quickly runne, hath this last pace,
My spans last inch, my minutes latest point,
And gluttonous death, will instantly unjoynt   5
My body, and soule, and I shall sleep a space,
But my'ever-waking part shall see that face,
Whose fear already shakes my every joynt:
Then, as my soule, to'heaven her first seate, takes flight,
And earth-borne body, in the earth shall dwell,   10
So, fall my sinnes, that all may have their right,
To where they'are bred, and would presse me, to hell,
Impute me righteous, thus purg'd of evill,
For thus I leave the world, the flesh, and devill.

Gerard Manley Hopkins, 'God's Grandeur' (1877, published 1918)

The world is charged with the grandeur of God.
   It will flame out, like shining from shook foil;
   It gathers to a greatness, like the ooze of oil
Crushed. Why do men then now not reck his rod?
Generations have trod, have trod, have trod;   5
   And all is seared with trade; bleared, smeared with toil;
   And wears man's smudge and shares man's smell: the soil
Is bare now, nor can foot feel, being shod.

And for all this, nature is never spent;
   There lives the dearest freshness deep down things;   10
And though the last lights off the black West went
   Oh, morning, at the brown brink eastward, springs –
Because the Holy Ghost over the bent
   World broods with warm breast and with ah! bright wings.

The sonnet offers the poet a particular kind of challenge. Its capacity for brief, emotionally charged and intensely organised statement has attracted the best poets and has produced great excellence. Each of these three poems, by acknowledged masters of the sonnet form, combines brevity of extent with expansiveness of philosophic reference. Each is concerned with a universal and apparently destructive process set against an assertion of its defeat, by art in the first, and religious conviction in the second and third. Each sonnet's content is organically related to its form.

Shakespeare's sonnet is composed of three quatrains plus a final couplet, rhyming *abab cdcd efef gg*, although the argument of the poem suggests a structure of twelve lines plus two. The three quatrains are clearly demarcated by stages in an argument and signalled by punctuation. An overt analogy (simile) in the first two lines compares a movement in the natural world with the shape of a human life. This is reinforced and elaborated in the second quatrain by a double focus on human and cosmic recession (it is impossible to find one word which adequately covers all of the senses Shakespeare requires here), maturity and decline. The third quatrain scrutinises the irresistible process of Time itself as a rhythm which underlies the preceding quatrains (in relation to youth and beauty), and concludes with the dissolution of all things. It is the closing couplet which provides a 'turn' away from the inevitability and conventionality of line 12, and it does so by directing the reader's mind to a consideration of the poem which he is reading. The fact that *reading* the poem as an artefact re-creates both its life and its subject's beauty means that it has escaped yet again the universal law of mortality. The celebration of youth and beauty through art is the only permanence, a triumph over death and despair.

The most remarkable feature of Donne's sonnet is its combination of fiercely energetic self-dramatisation perfectly allied with a coherence of form. All of Donne's sonnets carry a kind of desperate energy, a hope for salvation crossed with a corroding fear of damnation. And in common with most of the Holy Sonnets this one exploits two combined structures. The first is, quite clearly, the integral shape of the sonnet itself, and the second a particular discipline of meditation. This combination can be shown diagrammatically, as seen on p. 88. Within fourteen lines Donne refers to himself (*me/my/I*) fourteen times. He dramatises himself in order to analyse himself, or at least to spread his personal dilemma across the formal structure of evidence plus analysis plus proof (*This... And... Then... So... thus*). Within four lines only he uses five different methods of defining or measuring his progress towards death, and each moves from a whole to a component part (*play/scene; pilgrimage/last mile; race/last pace; span/last inch; minutes/latest point*), as if Donne is supplying in scientifically precise

The structure of Donne's 'Holy Sonnet' VI

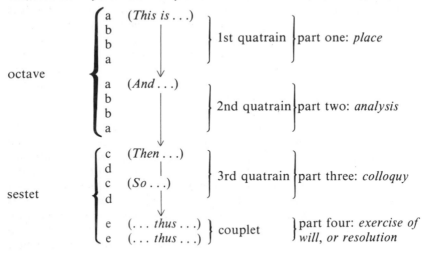

The structure of Shakespeare's Sonnet LX

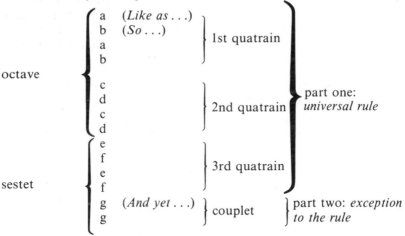

terms that sense of spiritual urgency which he as yet cannot feel on his pulses. The exclamatory and assertive verbal barrage (*is/hath/will/shall/already shakes*) evolves into doubt (*all may have/would presse me*) and imploring (*Impute me*) at the very moment when the need for certainty of salvation is at its most urgent.

If we compare this structure with Shakespeare's sonnet, an altogether different formal organisation emerges because Shakespeare has used both a different approach and a different purpose in the sonnet form. The movement of this poem may at first appear to be linear, that is it moves through three stages of an argument, which are thematically identical, to a conclusion. Yet the conclusion denies the validity of these three 'universal processes' and forces us to re-interpret the previous twelve lines as only partially true. Its argumentative shape is therefore circular. Unlike Donne's sonnet, it minimises the *argumentative* potential of the couplet and maximises the 'turn'.

The Hopkins sonnet is arranged, and spatially marked, as an octave and a sestet (8 + 6), rhyming *abba abba cdcdcd*, which immediately suggests a different movement from both the Shakespeare and the Donne examples. The 'turn' occurs at line 9, and is grammatically marked ('And for all this'). A blunt opening sentence states the sonnet's theme in a complete one-line unit. The question in line 4 as to why man is blind to God's immanence in nature is answered in lines 5 to 8, with emphatic devices such as monotonously heavy stresses, repetition, and assonantal links. Pessimism is turned aside in lines 9 and 10, and replaced by an image of cyclical renewal in both natural and spiritual worlds, thus providing a 'proof' of the assertion in the first line. It is therefore more clearly circular in its movement than Shakespeare's poem, though it lacks its continuous, wave-like motion. The pounding waves of the three quatrains are, as it were, resisted by the static shore-line of the couplet. We need no diagram to see that Hopkins's argument takes the shape of thesis + antithesis + synthesis.

Poetry in the making

D. H. Lawrence, 'Piano' (written *c.*1908–10, published 1918)

First draft:

Somewhere beneath that piano's superb sleek black
Must hide my mother's piano, little and brown, with the back
That stood close to the wall, and the front's faded silk both torn,
And the keys with little hollows, that my mother's fingers had worn.

Softly, in the shadows, a woman is singing to me   5
Quietly, through the years I have crept back to see
A child sitting under the piano, in the boom of the shaking strings
Pressing the little poised feet of the mother who smiles as she sings.

The full throated woman has chosen a winning, living song
And surely the heart that is in me must belong   10
To the Sunday evenings, when darkness wandered outside
And hymns gleamed on our warm lips, as we watched mother's
                                                    [fingers glide.

Or this is my sister at home in the old front room
Singing love's first surprised gladness, alone in the gloom.
She will start when she sees me, and blushing, spread out her
　　　　　　　　　　　　　　　　　　　　　[hands　　15
To cover my mouth's raillery, till I'm bound in her shame's heartspun
　　　　　　　　　　　　　　　　　　　　　　　[bands.

A woman is singing me a wild Hungarian air
And her arms, and her bosom, and the whole of her soul is bare,
And the great black piano is clamouring as my mother's never could
　　　　　　　　　　　　　　　　　　　　　[clamour
And my mother's tunes are devoured of this music's ravaging
　　　　　　　　　　　　　　　　　　　　　[glamour.　　20

Published version:

Softly, in the dusk, a woman is singing to me;
Taking me back down the vista of years, till I see
A child sitting under the piano, in the boom of the tingling strings
And pressing the small, posied feet of a mother who smiles as she
　　　　　　　　　　　　　　　　　　　　　[sings.

In spite of myself, the insidious mastery of song　　　　　　5
Betrays me back, till the heart of me weeps to belong
To the old Sunday evenings at home, with winter outside
And hymns in the cosy parlour, the tinkling piano our guide.

So now it is vain for the singer to burst into clamour
With the great black piano appassionato. The glamour　　　10
Of childish days is upon me, my manhood is cast
Down in the flood of remembrance, I weep like a child for the past.

The five-stanza poem precedes the three-stanza poem in order of
composition, and is the rejected first draft. The chief problem in both is
control of feeling and language in order to avoid sentimentality and
vagueness. Memories of childhood and a mother in conflict with the
sensual attractions of maturity, each linked in the poet's mind by music,
are the strands of a complex confession of defeat in both poems. But
only the second recognises and controls the conflict and the defeat. In
general, the revisions are of two kinds: formally, a greater precision, and
in terms of content, a greater self-awareness. The technique involved is
condensation (from five to three stanzas), and a greater organic control
of shape and language. If the first poem is cloying in its sentimentality
(particularly lines 4, 8, 12, the whole of stanza 4), then it is because there
is insufficient focus on the precise subject. The word 'little' in line 8 is
vague (Is the mother a midget?), whereas 'small' in the second version

implies something about size and something about grace and neatness also. 'Somewhere' (line 1) is vague and unhelpful; stanza four is signalled as an *additional* illustration of something already present in the poem ('Or this is . . .'). It is awkwardly phrased because it is cliché-ridden (What is 'love's first surprised gladness'?). The second version of the poem confronts the emotional vagueness and vigorously marks the entrapment in nostalgia and sentiment ('In spite of myself . . . insidious mastery . . . Betrays . . . it is vain . . . my manhood is cast/Down . . . I weep like a child'). In the second version 'glamour' is recognised for what it is, a superficially attractive image, but nevertheless an attractive one. Emotion misunderstood has defeated Lawrence in the first version, but in the second he has found the language to describe and animate his defeat.

The plot of the poem has also been reorganised. In the first, two pianos are juxtaposed, in a slightly ludicrous way. In the second, they are neatly linked through the title, object, sound and mood (*piano* = the musical direction 'softly'), thus also linking childhood and maturity, maternal and sensual attractions. In the first, it seems, Lawrence cannot make up his mind whether he is son or lover; in the second, the lover is seduced unwillingly by the son. The awkward contrast between the pianos on the one hand and the mother/woman/ Hungarian air on the other is deleted from the final version in favour of a precise confrontation of loyalties within the poet himself. Whereas the first poem seems to be an awkward formal combination of spreading rhythms of free verse shackled to a predetermined rhyme-scheme, the second moves easily and unobtrusively, each stanza being clearly separated and defined for a distinct purpose. 'Softly', 'In spite of myself', and 'So now it is vain' provide the syntactic outline of an inner conflict, whereas the first attempt is a jumble of directions.

In detail, word-choice shows an increasing economy and precision: 'shaking string' in the first version suggests only movement, whereas 'tingling strings' in the second combines movement *and* sound; 'childish' (line 11 of second version) is a pejorative term (cf. 'childlike', which is not) and clearly distances and defines at the same time; in the first version constructions such as 'surely . . . must' (line 10) and 'darkness wandered' (line 11), as well as 'gloom' (line 14) and 'shame's heartspun bands' (line 16) all indicate that the struggle for the right word has stopped short at cliché and vagueness.

Lawrence has made his poem no less personal in this process of revision. It is simply that he has worked into words a more precise and honest emotional feeling in relation to his subject. In this context it is useful to remind ourselves of the comment made by Paul Fussell in his *Poetic Meter and Poetic Form*:*

*Paul Fussell, *Poetic Meter and Poetic Form*, Random House, New York, 1965, p. 191.

poems are written not in the great outdoors where papers blow about and where one has no access to dictionaries, but at desks; their rhythms come as often from other poems as from the pulses of the poet; their stanzas are more frequently given the poet by history than supplied by momentary inspiration; and their varieties of logical organization are as artificial and labored over as the cornice of a stone building, or the nose of a statue in porphyry!

Elizabeth Jennings's poem 'Identity' captures in its opening lines the way a poet will hesitate in order to replace an ordinary word with its more precisely appropriate one:

> When I decide I shall assemble you
> Or, more precisely, when I decide which thoughts
> Of mine about you fit most easily together

Thomas Hardy's (1840–1928) poem 'At the Piano' (c. 1915) opens with a situation rather similar to Lawrence's 'Piano', but in the second stanza expresses in symbolic form a premonition of death:

> A woman was playing,
>   A man looking on;
>   And the mould of her face,
>   And her neck and her hair,
>   Which the rays fell upon
>   Of the two candles there,
> Sent him mentally straying
>   In some fancy-place
>   Where no pain had trace.
>
> A cowled Apparition
>   Came pushing between;
>   And her notes seemed to sigh;
>   And the lights to burn pale,
>   As a spell numbed the scene.
>   But the maid saw no bale,
> And the man no monition;
>   And Time laughed awry,
>   And the Phantom hid nigh.

Ted Hughes's poem 'The Thought-Fox' (1957) takes as its *subject* the process of poetic composition, and if we seek integrity of subject and image there are few more apt examples than this:

> I imagine this midnight moment's forest:
> Something else is alive
> Beside the clock's loneliness
> And this blank page where my fingers move.

Through the window I see no star:
Something more near
Though deeper within darkness
Is entering the loneliness:

Cold, delicately as the dark snow,
A fox's nose touches twig, leaf;
Two eyes serve a movement, that now
And again now, and now, and now

Sets neat prints into the snow
Between trees, and warily a lame
Shadow lags by stump and in hollow
Of a body that is bold to come

Across clearings, an eye,
A widening, deepening greenness,
Brilliantly, concentratedly,
Coming about its own business

Till, with a sudden sharp hot stink of fox
It enters the dark hole of the head.
The window is starless still; the clock ticks,
The page is printed.

For further reading, see Stephen Spender, 'The Making of a Poem', in Brewster Ghiselin, ed., *The Creative Process: A Symposium*, Mentor, New York, 1952, pp. 112–25, and A. F. Scott, *The Poet's Craft: A Course in the Critical Appreciation of Poetry*, Dover, New York, 1967 (first published by Cambridge University Press, 1967). This book contains many examples of manuscript poems and discusses their relationship with the printed versions.

Simplicity and significance

James Joyce, 'Ecce Puer' (1931)

Of the dark past
A child is born
With joy and grief
My heart is torn

Calm in his cradle
The living lies.
May love and mercy
Unclose his eyes!

5

Young life is breathed
On the glass   10
The world that was not
Comes to pass.

A child is sleeping:
An old man gone.
O, father forsaken,   15
Forgive your son!

W. B. Yeats, 'A Coat' (1914)

I made my song a coat
Covered with embroideries
Out of old mythologies
From heel to throat;
But the fools caught it,   5
Wore it in the world's eyes
As though they'd wrought it.
Song, let them take it,
For there's more enterprise
In walking naked.   10

Nothing is as difficult as writing simply. Both of these poems look simple and straightforward, and in some ways they are. The words all mean what they say, but additional meanings are implied by a sense that there is more here than meets the eye. The first poem is virtually monosyllabic, the second is *about* simplicity: both hinge on ambiguity, that is, the simultaneous plurality of meanings.

In form, the Joyce poem is four iambic dimeter quatrains rhyming *abcb*, a metrical structure which looks like and evokes in its rhythms the incantatory quality of a prayer or hymn. Its title might evoke the phrase 'Ecce Homo' ('Behold the Man'), of the Bible, John 19:5, used for a picture of Christ wearing the crown of thorns. Its last two lines might also evoke a biblical context: Matthew 27:46, 'My God, my God, why hast thou forsaken me' – Christ's words from the cross. We may know that Joyce wrote this poem on the birth of his grandson at the time of his own father's death, and interpret it as a private confession of joy at the first event, anguish at the second, each set into the context of the Christian relationship between God (Father), Christ (Son) and Man (grandchild). There is therefore a trinity of relationships *stated* and a Trinity of relationships evoked.

Structurally, the poem is built on contrasts which might be written out as follows:

birth–death
joy–grief
calm–dilemma
youth–age
being–extinction
sleep–death

and if we wished to provide a more specific context for the poem we might remember the parable of the Prodigal Son, or the final lines of the great medieval hymn, *Dies Irae*, translated as 'My God, my Father, and my Friend,/Do not forsake me in the End.'

In such ways Joyce's poem *suggests* spirals of meaning, because its personal and intimate references are set in the public language and context of Christian belief. What seems lexically simple spreads its significance into a universal pattern. Even so, the consummate art of this short poem is that it is perfectly satisfactory in its own terms whilst at the same time pregnant with evocations. The surface simplicity contains the potential for enrichment. What is personal becomes myth, and what was myth has been transformed into an intensely intimate experience.

In the Yeats poem the single image of a coat appears straightforward. Yeats is throwing off one style of poetry ('my song') in favour of another, since it has become common property. Lines 2 and 3 refer to Yeats's earlier use of 'decorative' imagery, from Celtic legend and myth, and the term 'naked' suggests that such things are now redundant to his needs and have become barriers not means to poetic expression. But the first line is ambiguous: a coat may conceal as well as identify, and Yeats may be saying that *either* his earlier poetry was a stylistic affectation, concealing his genuine 'voice', or that it was so 'exterior' and timely that it became too popular and was therefore taken over by others. In both senses Yeats resents what was once private having become public property. Popularity has submerged the individual voice.

If we compare the two poems we can discern two types of ambiguity. Joyce deftly evokes a parallel layer of significance, or rather, his own personal poem is penetrated throughout by a Christian analogy. Yeats's ambiguity is insolubly an ambiguousness of expression because of that single image and because of the syntax of the opening line (Is the song made *into* a coat, or is the coat made to *cover* the song?).

For further comparison with Joyce's poem, the following is one of many similar medieval carols (*c.*1500) in quatrains, which uses a conventional simile of sun shining through glass to describe the conception of Christ. It is noticeable, of course, that whereas the carol concentrates on maternity, Joyce concentrates his poem on paternity.

Synge we now both all and sum:
Christe redemtor omnium.

In Bethelem, that fayre cite,
Born was thys chylde so fayer and fre,
That Lorde and Kyng shal ever be,
A solis ortus cardine.

Ryght as the son shyneth on the glasse,
So Cryste Jesu in Owr Lady was;
Hym to sarve God sende us grace,
O lux beata Trinitas.

Cheldren were slayne grete plente,
Jesu Crist, all for the love of the;
Lorde, helpe us yf thy wyl it be.
Hostis Herodes impie.

Now ys he boren of Owr Lady,
The Son of the Fader that sytthyt an hye;
For owr synnys cry we all mercy,
Jesu salvator seculi.

The couplet

The main examples in this section are not taken from Pope, but it would be foolish to conceal his undisputed mastery of this poetic form. No poet has extracted more versatility from a single poetic line than Pope did from the iambic pentameter couplet. Here is one brief example of Pope's skill in matching form and content from 'Windsor Forest' (1713), embodying in form the idea of order in variety which Pope considers to be a political and social triumph of England under the reign of Queen Anne:

Here in full Light the russet Plains extend;
There wrapt in Clouds the blueish Hills ascend:

Here, diagrammatically, are the relationships contained within the couplet:

Place	Tone	Colour and perspective	Dimension
Hére	in full Líght	the rússet Pláins	exténd;
↕	↕	↕ ↕	↕
Thére	wrapt in Clóuds	the blueish Hílls	ascénd:

These two lines are metrically identical in form, but in every other way are dissimilar. By contrast, the *Epistle to Dr. Arbuthnot* (1731) draws our attention to the rhythm of spontaneous dialogue in such a way that the pentameter structure seems almost accidental, though of course it is not:

Shut, shut the door, good *John*! fatigu'd I said,
Tye up the knocker, say I'm sick, I'm dead,
The Dog-star rages! nay 'tis past a doubt,
All *Bedlam*, or *Parnassus*, is let out:
Fire in each eye, and Papers in each hand,
They rave, recite, and madden round the land.   (lines 1–6)

T. S. Eliot wrote what he thought was 'an excellent set of couplets' for
'The Fire Sermon' section of *The Waste Land*, based on Pope's *The Rape
of the Lock* (though much more like Swift's *Verses on the Death of Dr
Swift*). Eliot's Fresca, like Pope's Belinda, is a bored socialite. She opens
her morning letters and reads:

"My dear, how are you? I'm unwell today,
And have been, since I saw you at the play.
I hope that nothing mars your gaiety,
And things go better with you, than with me.
I went last night – more out of dull despair –
To Lady Kleinwurm's party – who was there?
Oh, Lady Kleinwurm's monde – no one that mattered –
Somebody sang, and Lady Kleinwurm chattered.
What are you reading? anything that's new?
I have a clever book by Giraudoux.
Clever, I think, is all. I've much to say –
But cannot say it – that is just my way –

The only comment necessary on these lines was reported by Eliot
himself. Ezra Pound remarked that 'Pope has done this so well that you
cannot do it better; and if you mean this as a burlesque, you had better
suppress it, for you cannot parody Pope unless you can write better verse
than Pope – and you can't.' Eliot deleted the passage from the published
version.*

The two examples of poetry in couplet form chosen here are from
Chaucer and from Dryden: both are verse-portraits, and both have a
satirical intention.

Geoffrey Chaucer, General Prologue to *The Canterbury Tales*, (?1478),
lines 118–62 (The Prioress)

Ther was also a Nonne, a PRIORESSE,
That of hir smyling was ful symple and coy;
Hire gretteste ooth was but by Seint Loy;
And she was cleped madame Eglentyne.
Ful weel she soong the service dyvyne,   5

* See Valerie Eliot, ed., *The Waste Land: A Facsimile and Transcript*, Faber & Faber,
London, 1971, pp. 23 and 127.

Entuned in hir nose ful semely,
And Frenssh she spak ful faire and fetisly,
After the scole of Stratford atte Bowe,
For Frenssh of Parys was to hire unknowe.
At mete wel ytaught was she withalle: 10
She let no morsel from hir lippes falle,
Ne wette hir fyngres in hir sauce depe;
Wel koude she carie a morsel and wel kepe
That no drope ne fille upon hir brest.
In curteisie was set ful muchel hir lest.   15
Hir over-lippe wyped she so clene
That in her coppe ther was no ferthyng sene
Of grece, whan she dronken hadde hir draughte.
Ful semely after hir mete she raughte.
And sikerly she was of greet desport,   20
And ful plesaunt, and amyable of port,
And peyned hire to countrefete cheere
Of court, and to been estatlich of manere,
And to ben holden digne of reverence.
But, for to speken of hire conscience,   25
She was so charitable and so pitous
She wolde wepe, if that she saugh a mous
Kaught in a trappe, if it were deed or bledde.
Of smale houndes hadde she that she fedde
With rosted flessh, or milk and wastel-breed.   30
But soore wepte she if oon of hem were deed,
Or if men smoot it with a yerde smerte;
And al was conscience and tendre herte.
Ful semyly hir wympul pynched was,
Hir nose tretys, hir eyen greye as glas,   35
Hir mouth ful smal, and thereto softe and reed;
But sikerly she hadde a fair forheed;
It was almoost a spanne brood, I trowe;
For, hardily, she was nat undergrowe.
Ful fetys was hir cloke, as I was war.   40
Of smal coral aboute hire arm she bar
A peire of bedes, gauded al with grene,
And theron heng a brooch of gold ful sheene,
On which ther was first write a crowned A,
And after *Amor vincit omnia.**   45

* NOTES: line 8, *Stratford atte Bowe*, i.e. the Prioress's French had been learnt at a
nunnery, not in France; line 17, *ferthyng*, trace; line 19, her table-manners were
impeccable; line 30, *wastel-breed*, fine white bread; line 32, *yerde*, stick; line 35, *tretys*,
straight.

John Dryden, *Absalom and Achitophel* (1681), lines 543–68, the character of Zimri (i.e. George Villiers, Duke of Buckingham)*

Some of their Chiefs were Princes of the Land:
In the first Rank of these did *Zimri* stand:
A man so various, that he seem'd to be
Not one, but all Mankind's Epitome.
Stiff in Opinions, always in the wrong;   5
Was every thing by starts, and nothing long:
But, in the course of one revolving Moon,
Was Chymist, Fidler, States-Man, and Buffoon:
Then all for Women, Painting, Rhiming, Drinking;
Besides ten thousand freaks that dy'd in thinking.   10
Blest Madman, who could every hour employ,
With something New to wish, or to enjoy!
Rayling and praising were his usual Theams;
And both (to show his Judgment) in Extreams:
So over Violent, or over Civil,   15
That every man, with him, was God or Devil.
In squandering Wealth was his peculiar Art:
Nothing went unrewarded, but Desert.
Begger'd by Fools, whom still he found too late:
He had his Jest, and they had his Estate.   20
He laught himself from Court, then sought Relief
By forming Parties, but could ne'er be Chief:
For, spight of him, the weight of Business fell
On *Absalom* and wise *Achitophel*:
Thus, wicked but in will, of means bereft,   25
He left not Faction, but of that was left.

Experts still debate Chaucer's metrical characteristics, since there is no certainty about how his lines were performed. What is certain is that Chaucer's poetry was written to be performed by the speaking voice and that his poetry enacts exactly the same relationship between *metrical paradigm* and performance rules as any other poet's work. Chaucer's

* The Duke of Buckingham, was chief minister of Charles II from 1667 to 1674, but thereafter was associated with the Whigs. Dryden's portrait in verse may be compared with Bishop Burnet's prose sketch in *History of my Own Times* (1724–53): 'He had a great liveliness of wit, and a peculiar faculty of turning all things into ridicule: . . . he was drawn into chymistry: And for some years he thought he was very near the finding the philosopher's stone. He had no principles of religion, vertue, or friendship. Pleasure, frolick, or extravagant diversion was all that he laid to heart. He was true to nothing, for he was not true to himself. He had no steadiness nor conduct . . . He could never fix his thoughts, nor govern his estate, tho' then the greatest in *England*.'

metre was not understood from the sixteenth century until the last quarter of the eighteenth century, when Tyrwhitt's edition appeared. For example, the final *e* in *mete* (line 10) is stressed, and the word therefore has two syllables, as has *depe* (line 12). Chaucer's vocabulary is heavily penetrated by French loan words, so that *conscience* (line 25) and *charitable* (line 26) would be stressed on the *third* syllable (and on the first, as in modern English), and in both cases the final *e* would carry a stress also.

The remarkable subtlety of Chaucer's portrait of the Prioress lies in what he *does not* say about her. If we deleted the word PRIORESSE we should be left with a portrait of a socially accomplished and romantically beautiful woman of refined sensibility and exquisite manners. Strictly speaking, the Prioress should not have been on a pilgrimage at all, should not have owned dogs, and should not have taken such pains to stress her physical beauty. Her fastidiousness at table and her emotional sensitivity to the suffering of animals are both admirable, but one then asks the question: Does the Prioress's concern for ritual *forms* (religious and social) take precedence over her proper spiritual and human concerns? Chaucer permits hints of ambiguity throughout this portrait, but at no point clearly suggests that her sensuality and sophistication are actually blameworthy. Like Pope's portrait of Belinda in Canto II of *The Rape of the Lock*, the impression of praise and compliment almost conceals an undercurrent of blame. Beneath the finery, there is a charge that sticks: the materialism of the Church establishment has become *self*-centred, more concerned with worldly appearance than with spiritual function.

Chaucer thinks in terms of a whole paragraph of verse, building up the portrait to an ambiguous climax in the last line. The relationship between rhyme and meaning within the couplets is not, perhaps, more than a principle of construction, since it is the *total* effect of many details at which Chaucer is aiming. Much of the description of her physical beauty is borrowed (from *The Romance of the Rose*, and from a context concerned with sexual attraction), and the question, again, is the appropriateness of it. In spite of what commentators may say, the modern reader cannot avoid the suspicion that *countrefete* (22), if not *coy* (2), plus the frequent stress on *semely* and the synonymous *fetisly*, in lines 6, 7, 19, 34, 40 are ironic both in intention and effect. Chaucer's eyebrow is lifted in both admiration and quizzical surprise, and the final line is packed with ambiguity. If Love conquers all, it may be God's love or the love of man; it may also be sensual love, and it may be Chaucer's own insinuation that, in Pope's words, 'If to her share some female errors fall,/Look on her face, and you'll forget them all.'

In Dryden's hands the rhyming couplet becomes a surgical implement for satirical anatomy. Each formal and structural potential is utilized, like a stiletto, to inflict a neat but nevertheless mortal wound. The best introduction to this portrait and to its method is Dryden's own remarks in *A Discourse Concerning the Original and Progress of Satire* (1693), where he describes the distinction between 'fine raillery' and mere invective:

> How easy is it to call rogue and villain, and that wittily! But how hard to make a man appear a fool, a blockhead, or a knave without using any of those opprobrious terms! To spare the grossness of the names, and to do the thing yet more severely, is to draw a full face, and to make the nose and cheeks stand out, and yet not to employ any depth of shadowing... A witty man is tickled while he is hurt in this manner, and a fool feels it not... there is still a vast difference betwixt the slovenly butchering of man, and the fineness of a stroke that separates the head from the body, and leaves it standing in its place... The character of Zimri in my *Absalom* is, in my opinion, worth the whole poem: it is not bloody, but it is ridiculous enough; and he, for whom it was intended, was too witty to resent it as an injury. If I had railed, I might have suffered for it justly; but I managed my own work more happily, perhaps more dexterously. I avoided the mention of great crimes, and applied myself to the representing of blindsides, and little extravagancies; to which, the wittier a man is, he is generally the more obnoxious. It succeeded as I wished; the jest went round, and he was laughed at in his turn who began the frolic.

Dryden's portrait is of a type, the Inconstant Man, normally ridiculous but nevertheless dangerous if he bids for high public office. The poetry creates as well as demolishes its subject, decapitating without butchering its target, fabricating a dazzling energy without purpose and a comic schizophrenia. The tendency of the couplet towards epigrammatic statement provides a semantic box, a kind of verbal strait-jacket for its lunatic subject. Lines 7 and 8, for example, unite rhyme to meaning in a functional link associating the phases of the moon (lunar) to the revolutions of an unstable personality (lunatic), whilst the list itself, 'Chymist, Fidler, States-Man, and Buffoon' suggests that these normally highly disparate activities are more than syntactically of the same *value* in its subject's personality. The last item in this list is both a climax and a qualification of all the other items. By comparison with Chaucer, Dryden's *local* effects (as distinct from the paragraph as a whole) are more sharply satirical although equally a matter of details in a whole. Its style is parenthetical, with clauses interrupting sentences, and the caesural variation is used with a satirical function (as in lines 5 and 6, 19 and 20, and 25 and 26), often providing a witty 'turn' by reversing or subverting any impression of continuity or stability. Chaucer insinuates a critical commentary through the use of ambiguities and by *not* saying the expected; Dryden deflates Zimri's importance by overt ridicule, and the fun provided by the poetry defuses its subject's claim to serious attention.

Poetry and belief

William Blake, 'The Garden of Love' (from *Songs of Experience*, 1789–94)

I went to the Garden of Love,
And saw what I never had seen:
A Chapel was built in the midst,
Where I used to play on the green.

And the gates of this Chapel were shut,   5
And 'Thou shalt not' writ over the door;
So I turn'd to the Garden of Love
That so many sweet flowers bore;

And I saw it was filled with graves,
And tomb-stones where flowers should be;   10
And Priests in black gowns were walking their rounds,
And binding with briars my joys & desires.

Thomas Hardy, 'The Impercipient (At a Cathedral Service)' (1898)

That with this bright believing band
    I have no claim to be,
That faiths by which my comrades stand
    Seem fantasies to me,
And mirage-mists their Shining Land,   5
    Is a strange destiny.

Why thus my soul should be consigned
    To infelicity,
Why always I must feel as blind
    To sights my brethren see,   10
Why joys they've found I cannot find,
    Abides a mystery.

Since heart of mine knows not that ease
    Which they know; since it be
That He who breathes All's Well to these   15
    Breathes no All's Well to me,
My lack might move their sympathies
    And Christian charity!

I am like a gazer who should mark
    An inland company   20
Standing upfingered, with, 'Hark! hark!
    The glorious distant sea!'
And feel, 'Alas, 'tis but yon dark
    And wind-swept pine to me!'

Yet I would bear my shortcomings   25
    With meet tranquillity,
But for the charge that blessed things
    I'd liefer not have be.
O, doth a bird deprived of wings
    Go earth-bound wilfully!   30

       ★   ★   ★   ★

Enough. As yet disquiet clings
    About us. Rest shall we.

In both of these poems the voice we hear is that of an 'outsider'. Blake thinks in symbolic terms, Hardy starts from a specific experience (the original title of Hardy's poem was 'The Agnostic (Evensong: – Cathedral)', and in *Wessex Poems* he provided a sketch of the nave of Salisbury Cathedral during a religious service). In both poems the institutional church fails to satisfy the individual's spiritual needs. Whereas Blake feels excluded from a spiritual home he once knew, Hardy's sense of isolation from the 'bright believing band' produces a sense of personal and irresolvable inadequacy. A link between the two poems is suggested by Wordsworth's *Ode: Intimations of Immortality* (1807):

But trailing clouds of glory do we come
    From God who is our home:
Heaven lies about us in our infancy!
Shades of the prison-house begin to close
    Upon the growing Boy.   (lines 65–9)

Repression and spiritual death pervade Blake's poem, contrasted with the spontaneous freedom suggested by childhood and natural imagery. Hardy turns the official messages of consolation ('All's Well') into a hollow mockery of his own spiritual doubt. Each is exiled, both feel resentment. But Blake's degree of resentment is greater than Hardy's, though less personal. The final stanza of 'The Garden of Love' implies through images the idea that the Church has stultified growth and brought death to that which is by nature joyous. Ritual has killed both spiritual and natural love, a point which Hardy makes more clearly than in 'The Impercipient' in his poem 'God's Funeral' (1908–10):

> And they composed a crowd of whom
> Some were right good, and many nigh the best . . . .
> Thus dazed and puzzled, 'twixt the gleam and gloom
> Mechanically I followed with the rest

an example of what Hardy termed 'the forced adaptation of human instincts to rusty and irksome moulds that do not fit them' (1912 postscript to his novel *Jude the Obscure*). The poetic form of 'The Impercipient' (six-line iambic tetrameters, with a final rhymed couplet) offers Hardy's alternative hymn of doubt in a context of public certainty. It adopts the form and conventional *imagery* of many hymns: compare Hardy's fourth and fifth stanzas with the first two stanzas of the hymn 'Hark! a thrilling voice is sounding':

> Hark! a thrilling voice is sounding;
>   'Christ is nigh,' it seems to say;
> 'Cast away the dreams of darkness,
>   O ye children of the day!'

> Wakened by the solemn warning,
>   Let the earth-bound soul arise;
> Christ, her Sun, all ill dispelling,
>   Shines upon the morning skies.

Hardy's poetic form is thus a significant part of the poem's theme of private doubt: it subverts the hymn-form rather like a critical commentary on a text.

For further reading see A. S. P. Woodhouse, *The Poet and his Faith: Religion and Poetry in England from Spenser to Eliot and Auden*, Chicago University Press, Chicago and London, 1965.

The poet's voice

William Blake, Introduction to *Songs of Experience* (1794)

> Hear the voice of the Bard!
> Who Present, Past, & Future, sees,
> Whose ears have heard
> The Holy Word,
> That walk'd among the ancient trees,   5

> Calling the lapsed Soul,
> And weeping in the evening dew;
> That might controll
> The starry pole;
> And fallen, fallen light renew!   10

'O Earth, O Earth, return!
'Arise from out the dewy grass;
'Night is worn,
'And the morn
'Rises from the slumberous mass.   15

'Turn away no more;
'Why wilt thou turn away?
'The starry floor,
'The wat'ry shore,
'Is giv'n thee till the break of day.'   20

T. S. Eliot, from *The Waste Land* (1922), lines 215–65

At the violet hour, when the eyes and back
Turn upward from the desk, when the human engine waits
Like a taxi throbbing waiting,
I Tiresias, though blind, throbbing between two lives,
Old man with wrinkled female breasts, can see   5
At the violet hour, the evening hour that strives
Homeward, and brings the sailor home from sea,
The typist home at teatime, clears her breakfast, lights
Her stove, and lays out food in tins.
Out of the window perilously spread   10
Her drying combinations touched by the sun's last rays.
On the divan are piled (at night her bed)
Stockings, slippers, camisoles, and stays.
I Tiresias, old man with wrinkled dugs
Perceived the scene, and foretold the rest –   15
I too awaited the expected guest.
He, the young man carbuncular, arrives,
A small house agent's clerk, with one bold stare,
One of the low on whom assurance sits
As a silk hat on a Bradford millionaire.   20
The time is now propitious, as he guesses,
The meal is ended, she is bored and tired,
Endeavours to engage her in caresses
Which still are unreproved, if undesired.
Flushed and decided, he assaults at once;   25
Exploring hands encounter no defence;
His vanity requires no response,
And makes a welcome of indifference.
(And I Tiresias have foresuffered all
Enacted on this same divan or bed;   30
I who have sat by Thebes below the wall

And walked among the lowest of the dead.)
Bestows one final patronizing kiss,
And gropes his way, finding the stairs unlit . . .

She turns and looks a moment in the glass,   35
Hardly aware of her departed lover;
Her brain allows one half-formed thought to pass;
'Well now that's done: and I'm glad it's over.'
When lovely woman stoops to folly and
Paces about her room again, alone,   40
She smoothes her hair with automatic hand,
And puts a record on the gramophone.

'This music crept by me upon the waters'
And along the Strand, up Queen Victoria Street.
O City city, I can sometimes hear   45
Beside a public bar in Lower Thames Street,
The pleasant whining of a mandoline
And a clatter and a chatter from within
Where fishmen lounge at noon: where the walls
of Magnus Martyr hold   50
Inexplicable splendour of Ionian white and gold

In each of these poems the poet adopts a public persona, or dramatic
character, through whom a prophetic message is uttered. Blake's bard
has his origins in oral poetry, where the poet is the repository of tribal
wisdom and history, who enacts the moral and religious values of the
past as a guide to the future. Thomas Gray's scholarly research into
Welsh history permeates his poem 'The Bard' (1757), and he depicts the
bard as a part of elemental nature (here prophesying the downfall of
Edward I's dynasty and the triumph of the House of Tudor):

On a rock, whose haughty brow
Frowns o'er old Conway's foaming flood,
Robed in the sable garb of woe,
With haggard eyes the Poet stood;
(Loose his beard, and hoary hair
Stream'd, like a meteor, to the troubled air)
And with a Master's hand, and Prophet's fire,
Struck the deep sorrows of his lyre.

Eliot's Tiresias, described in a note as 'the most important personage in
the poem', is borrowed from Greek mythology. In one version, Tiresias
is blinded for having seen Athene (the Greek goddess of wisdom,
industry and war and daughter of Zeus, the greatest of the Greek gods)
bathing, but in the version preferred by Eliot, Tiresias is blinded by Hera
(the jealous consort of Zeus, protectress of marriage) because he agreed

with Zeus's opinion that men derive more pleasure from love than women. Transformed for a time into a woman, Tiresias is subsequently given long life and the gift of prophecy by Zeus. Tennyson's Tiresias is cursed for having experienced Athene's naked beauty:

'Henceforth be blind, for thou hast seen too much,
And speak the truth that no man may believe.'

Both versions fit Eliot's theme of an anti-romantic present, passionless, mechanical, and spiritually dead, existing unaware of the links with a magnificent past. The 'splendour' of the 'Ionian white and gold' is not merely an architectural feature of the church mentioned in the preceding line, but an evocation of a period characterised by cultural achievement married to spiritual aspiration. From his vantage-point outside time, the pained Tiresias both sympathises with and laments the perpetual cycle of sensuality which is only sex, and life degenerated to routine.

Blake's bard, similarly, reminds his audience of their spiritual obligations, but through a direct exhortation. His voice is unlimited by time and space: it is the voice of Revelation and warning, extending hope and fear at the same time. Metrically, and by comparison with Eliot's poem, Blake's poem is straightforward (four iambic cinquains rhyming *abaab*, but varying stresses within the lines from two to four, with marked trochaic substitution in lines 1, 6, 15 and 16, and with pararhyme (Bard/beard)). Eliot's poem may read like blank verse, but is in fact an extraordinary mixture of regularity and irregularity.

This 51-line passage has an average of between four and five stresses per line and a mixture of rhymed and unrhymed groups of lines, as follows (rhymes are marked in separate groupings, and do not relate to recurrent rhymes across the whole passage):

1–3	unrhymed
4–7	quatrain (*abab*)
8–9	unrhymed
10–13	quatrain (*abab*)
14	unrhymed
15–16	couplet (*aa*)
17–20	'irregular quatrain' (*abcb*)
21–4	quatrain (*abab*)
25–8	quatrain (*abab*)
29–32	quatrain (*abab*)
33–4	unrhymed
35–8	quatrain (*abab*)
39–42	quatrain (*abab*)
43–6	'irregular' quatrain (*abcb*, as above: but note Street/Street)
47–8	couplet (*aa*)
49–51	couplet (*aa*), but arranged as three lines

The passage is also punctuated (lines 4, 14, 16, 29, 31) with Tiresias interposing himself into the scene, providing a rhythmic penetration and a chorus. But what are we to make of the passage's unusual and apparently whimsical combination of blank verse and rhyme? Do its fractured rhythms and broken continuities relate to meaning? Are we aware, as we read it, that each of the quatrains contains a complete statement, or marks an individual scene, or describes a particular character or event, or that when Tiresias talks of himself (lines 29–32) he does so in a rhymed pentameter quatrain? Are we to hear the echo of the 'heroic' line ironically counterpointing a modern mockery of romantic love? It is impossible to read beyond lines 10–11 without experiencing Eliot's ironic juxtapositioning of what is with what we might expect. This is no daughter of Zeus undressing, nor is the spotty young man interested in her beauty, least of all in making a conquest. In short, the metrical characteristics of this passage are *functionally* related to its meaning, breaking expectations, clashing form and content, interrupting rhythmic patterning, and producing a jerky sense of mock-romantic frustration. Metrical choice thus underpins the poet's meaning.

For further reading see Blake's 'Earth's Answer' (*Songs of Experience*), 'The Voice of the Ancient Bard' (*Songs of Innocence*), Gray's 'The Fatal Sisters. An Ode'.

Blank verse

George Gordon, Lord Byron, *Darkness* (1816)

I had a dream, which was not all a dream.
The bright sun was extinguished, and the stars
Did wander darkling in the eternal space,
Rayless, and pathless, and the icy earth
Swung blind and blackening in the moonless air;   5
Morn came and went – and came, and brought no day,
And men forgot their passions in the dread
Of this their desolation; and all hearts
Were chilled into a selfish prayer for light:
And they did live by watchfires – and the thrones,   10
The palaces of crowned kings – the huts,
The habitations of all things which dwell,
Were burnt for beacons; cities were consumed,
And men gathered round their blazing homes
To look once more into each other's face;   15
Happy were those who dwelt within the eye
Of the volcanoes, and their mountain torch:

A fearful hope was all the world contained;
Forests were set on fire – but hour by hour
They fell and faded – and the crackling trunks   20
Extinguished with a crash – and all was black.
The brows of men by the despairing light
Wore an unearthly aspect, as by fits
The flashes fell upon them; some lay down
And hid their eyes and wept; and some did rest   25
Their chins upon their clenched hands, and smiled;
And others hurried to and fro, and fed
Their funeral piles with fuel, and looked up
With mad disquietude on the dull sky,
The pall of a past world; and then again   30
With curses cast them down upon the dust,
And gnashed their teeth and howled: the wild birds shrieked
And, terrified, did flutter on the ground,
And flap their useless wings; the wildest brutes
Came tame and tremulous; and vipers crawled   35
And twined themselves among the multitude,
Hissing, but stingless – they were slain for food;
And War, which for a moment was no more,
Did glut himself again: – a meal was bought
With blood, and each sate sullenly apart   40
Gorging himself in gloom: no love was left;
All earth was but one thought – and that was death
Immediate and inglorious; and the pang
Of famine fed upon all entrails – men
Died, and their bones were tombless as their flesh;   45
The meagre by the meagre were devoured,
Even dogs assailed their masters, all save one,
And he was faithful to a corse, and kept
The birds and beasts and famished men at bay,
Till hunger clung them, or the dropping dead   50
Lured their lank jaws; himself sought out no food,
But with a piteous and perpetual moan,
And a quick desolate cry, licking the hand
Which answered not with a caress – he died.
The crowd was famished by degrees; but two   55
Of an enormous city did survive,
And they were enemies: they met beside
The dying embers of an altar-place
Where had been heaped a mass of holy things
For an unholy usage; they raked up,   60
And shivering scraped with their cold skeleton hands

The feeble ashes, and their feeble breath
Blew for a little life, and made a flame
Which was a mockery; then they lifted up
Their eyes as it grew lighter, and beheld   65
Each other's aspects – saw, and shrieked, and died –
Even of their mutual hideousness they died,
Unknowing who he was upon whose brow
Famine had written Fiend. The world was void,
The populous and the powerful was a lump   70
Seasonless, herbless, treeless, manless, lifeless –
A lump of death – a chaos of hard clay.
The rivers, lakes, and ocean all stood still,
And nothing stirred within their silent depths;
Ships sailorless lay rotting on the sea,   75
And their masts fell down piecemeal: as they dropped
They slept on the abyss without a surge –
The waves were dead; the tides were in their grave,
The Moon, their mistress, had expired before;
The winds were withered in the stagnant air,   80
And the clouds perished; Darkness had no need
Of aid from them – She was the Universe.

Byron imagines the end of life on earth, as a dream. At the end of the
New Testament is the Book of Revelation, St John's apocalyptic vision
of universal catastrophe visited upon a sinful world by fire, plague,
earthquake, cosmic collisions, hailstorms, firestorms, a plague of
locusts, the cessation of winds, the extinction of the sun, and a sea which
has turned to blood (Revelation 8–16). Byron makes no mention of the
catastrophe as a Divine punishment, and for twentieth-century readers
confronted with the threat of a nuclear holocaust Byron's poem is not so
much a nightmare as an omen. Its meaning is clear enough. What we
should also enquire about is its poetic method, its structure, and its
shape.
    It is written in unrhymed iambic pentameters (blank verse), the metre
of Shakespeare's plays, Milton's *Paradise Lost*, Wordsworth's *The
Prelude*, the monologues (for example, 'Andrea del Sarto', 1855) of
Robert Browning (1812–89), and Yeats's plays. Apart from its opening
line, a complete verse and grammatical unit, there are only four
sentences (lines 2–21, 22–54, 55–69, 69–82) in an eighty-two line poem.
What, then, are its structuring methods, since it dispenses with the local
structuring device of rhyme? The only comment we can make about its
total shape is that it is a *verse paragraph*, but within this shape there are
at least seven types of structuring device, apart from the obvious use of
'and' (fifty-six occurrences):

(1) *adjectival pairing:* 'Rayless and pathless' (4), 'Immediate and inglorious' (43), 'piteous and perpetual' (52), for example. Each includes either alliteration or assonance as a phonetic linkage.

(2) *verbal pairing:* 'came and went' (6), 'fell and faded' (20).

(3) *noun pairing:* 'birds and beasts' (49, alliterative).

(4) *alliterative lines:* 'Gorging himself in gloom: no *l*ove was *l*eft' (41).

(5) *verbal sequences:* 'saw, and shrieked, and died' (66).

(6) *adjectival sequences:* 'Seasonless, herbless, treeless, manless, lifeless' (71).

(7) *repetition with variation:* 'Morn came and went – and came, and brought no day' (6).

Between lines there is alliterative linkage, as in 50–1, 'dropping dead/Lured their lank...'; run-on lines are frequent, and full stops occur within the body of the poem on what might be called the 'load-bearing' words, 'black' (21), 'died' (54), 'Fiend' (69), and, finally, 'Universe' (82). If we look at the vocabulary of the poem we shall observe that Byron varies three basic semantic areas, death, darkness and famine:

death	darkness	famine
funeral piles (28)	*darkling* (3)	*famine* (44)
death (42, 72)	*Rayless* (4)	*famished* (49, 55)
men/Died (44–5)	*black* (21)	*hunger* (50)
dropping dead (50)	*gloom* (41)	*no food* (51)
he died (54)	*pall* (30)	*Famine* (69)
corse (i.e. corpse, (48))	*blind and blackening* (5)	*withered* (80)
dying embers (58)	*moonless* (5)	
skeleton hands (61)	*no day* (6)	
died (54, 66, 67)	*despairing light* (22)	
dead (78)	*extinguished* (2)	
in their grave (78)	*Extinguished* (21)	
expired (79)		
perished (81)		

In a poem about dissolution we would, of course, expect frequent use to be made of such terms, but all of these terms seem to converge upon the lines

Seasonless, herbless, treeless, manless, lifeless –
A lump of death – a chaos of hard clay.

The *negatives* in these lines are obvious enough, but they only bring to a climax an insistent negativity throughout the entire poem, no single item of which is repeated: *Rayless, pathless* (4), *moonless* (5), *no day* (6), *unearthly* (23), *useless* (34), *stingless* (37), *no more* (38), *no love* (41), *tombless* (45), *no food* (51), *not with a caress* (54), *unholy* (60), *Unknowing*

(68), *nothing* (74), *sailorless* (75), *without* (77), *no need* (81). It is the interpenetration of these words which produces a terrifying intensity of vision and a remorselessness of concentration. This also means that the structural organisation of the whole paragraph is extremely tight: it proceeds without pause or relief by an accumulation of cross-referred details to its catastrophic climax. A sense of inevitability is felt at the end, for the whole poem's cumulative weight bears down upon it. An internal pattern of rhyming units would have produced additional, if not different effects, but would have certainly decorated the poem with a spurious elegance. We might ask, then, why Byron chose not to write in the ultimately much more flexible form of 'free verse'. Historically, of course, such a form did not exist until much later in the nineteenth century, but the answer must surely lie in the satisfaction to be gained within an existing form. There is no terminal rhyme in blank verse, but the terminal *words* (certainly in this poem) set up reverberations between the lines. Consider the terminally stressed words in the first eleven lines (*dream, stars, space, earth, air, day, dread, hearts, light, thrones, huts*), all key words in Byron's dream of cosmic chaos and human disorder. The last two (*thrones, huts*) suggest by word order alone the levelling process of death itself. Now none of these structural devices exists to compensate for the absence of rhyme: had Byron needed rhyme, there is nothing either in the subject or treatment to prevent its use. But for some poets, blank verse is deficient for certain effects. Tennyson remarked on the difficulty of describing commonplace objects in blank verse without sacrificing 'poetical elevation'. Keats gave the opposite reason for abandoning his blank verse epic *Hyperion*:

> I have given up Hyperion . . . Miltonic verse cannot be written but in an artful or rather artist's humour. I wish to give myself up to other sensations. English ought to be kept up. It may be interesting to you to pick out some lines from Hyperion and put a mark X to the false beauty proceeding from art, and one ‖ to the true voice of feeling.
>
> (Letter to Reynolds, 21 September 1819)

A similar argument is provided by T. S. Eliot in relation to Yeats's plays in blank verse:

> When he first began to write plays, poetic drama meant plays written in blank verse. Now, blank verse has been a dead metre for a long time . . . it is obvious that a form which was handled so supremely well by Shakespeare has its disadvantages. If you are writing a play of the same type as Shakespeare's, the reminiscence is oppressive; if you are writing a play of a different type, it is distracting . . . blank verse can hardly be dissociated from the life of the sixteenth and seventeenth centuries: it can hardly catch the rhythms with which English is spoken nowadays.   (First Annual Yeats lecture, Dublin, 1940)

Clearly, the anxiety of influence is a strong deterrent. Shakespeare and Milton, it seems, have temporarily taken possession of the blank verse line and by their example prevented others from using it.

As Eliot himself points out in the same lecture, the re-establishment of blank verse is possible in time, 'during the course of which it will have liberated itself from period associations'. Wordsworth's greatest poem, *The Prelude*, is not diminished by its Miltonic echoes, nor do we feel that its blank verse in some way competes with the form of *Paradise Lost*. In the *Lyrical Ballads* volume (1798) Wordsworth had tried an experiment 'to ascertain, how far, by fitting to metrical arrangement a selection of the real language of men in a state of vivid sensation, that sort of pleasure and that quantity of pleasure may be imparted, which a Poet may rationally endeavour to impart'. His theory of poetry eschews narrow formal definition in favour of psychological intention: 'the primary laws of our nature'. Thus the twelfth book of *The Prelude* is entitled 'Imagination and Taste, How Impaired and Restored', and the following passage argues that ordinary experience may be endowed by the poet with great significance and that the operation of the poet's mind on that experience defines his creative sensibility. The 'poetry' is not in the language or the metrical shape but in the nature of the experience.

From William Wordsworth's *The Prelude* (written 1798–1805; published 1850), Book XII, lines 208–86

    There are in our existence spots of time,
That with distinct pre-eminence retain
A renovating virtue, whence, depressed
By false opinion and contentious thought,
Or aught of heavier or more deadly weight,   5
In trivial occupations, and the round
Of ordinary intercourse, our minds
Are nourished and invisibly repaired;
A virtue, by which pleasure is enhanced,
That penetrates, enables us to mount,   10
When high, more high, and lifts us up when fallen.
This efficacious spirit chiefly lurks
Among those passages of life that give
Profoundest knowledge to what point, and how,
The mind is lord and master – outward sense   15
The obedient servant of her will. Such moments
Are scattered everywhere, taking their date
From our first childhood. I remember well,
That once, while yet my inexperienced hand
Could scarcely hold a bridle, with proud hopes   20

I mounted, and we journeyed towards the hills:
An ancient servant of my father's house
Was with me, my encourager and guide:
We had not travelled long, ere some mischance
Disjoined me from my comrade; and, through fear   25
Dismounting, down the rough and stony moor
I led my horse, and, stumbling on, at length
Came to a bottom, where in former times
A murderer had been hung in iron chains.
The gibbet-mast had mouldered down, the bones   30
And iron case were gone; but on the turf,
Hard by, soon after that fell deed was wrought,
Some unknown hand had carved the murderer's name.
The monumental letters were inscribed
In times long past; but still, from year to year,   35
By superstition of the neighbourhood,
The grass is cleared away, and to this hour
The characters are fresh and visible:
A casual glance had shown them, and I fled,
Faltering and faint, and ignorant of the road: 40
Then, reascending the bare common, saw
A naked pool that lay beneath the hills,
The beacon of the summit, and, more near,
A girl, who bore a pitcher on her head,
And seemed with difficult steps to force her way   45
Against the blowing wind. It was, in truth,
An ordinary sight; but I should need
Colours and words that are unknown to man,
To paint the visionary dreariness
Which, while I looked all round for my lost guide,   50
Invested moorland waste, and naked pool,
The beacon crowning the lone eminence,
The female and her garments vexed and tossed
By the strong wind. When, in the blessed hours
Of early love, the loved one at my side,   55
I roamed, in daily presence of this scene,
Upon the naked pool and dreary crags,
And on the melancholy beacon, fell
A spirit of pleasure and youth's golden gleam;
And think ye not with radiance more sublime   60
For these remembrances, and for the power
They had left behind? So feeling comes in aid
Of feeling, and diversity of strength
Attends us, if but once we have been strong.

Oh! mystery of man, from what a depth   65
Proceed thy honours. I am lost, but see
In simple childhood something of the base
On which thy greatness stands; but this I feel,
That from thyself it comes, that thou must give,
Else never canst receive. The days gone by   70
Return upon me almost from the dawn
Of life: the hiding-places of man's power
Open; I would approach them, but they close.
I see by glimpses now; when age comes on,
May scarcely see at all; and I would give,   75
While yet we may, as far as words can give,
Substance and life to what I feel, enshrining,
Such is my hope, the spirit of the Past
For future restoration. –

The structure of this verse paragraph is determined from within. Whereas the Byron example is packed with linkages within, across and throughout the verse paragraph, generating great concentration of mood by a narrow semantic range, Wordsworth's writing is discursive and moves from philosophic statement (1–16), by way of transition (16–18), to example in narrative form (18–46), to reflection on the significance of the narrative (46–62), and finally to an elevated and intensely personal meditation on the whole episode. Wordsworth is recollecting a past incident in the present, one of those luminous but in themselves commonplace incidents of childhood from which he draws poetic sustenance, and to which he may return for inspiration in moments of creative depression. It is therefore not simply a *stylistic* point that this passage is markedly parenthetical. If Wordsworth looks to his early life for inspiration as a mature poet, then the former is in fact 'contained' within the latter. Most of lines 3–7 are embedded within the enclosing structure of the sentence in lines 1–3, 7–8:

> There are in our existence spots of time,
> That with distinct pre-eminence retain
> A renovating virtue, whence . . .
>   . . . our minds
> Are nourished and invisibly repaired;

Because of this parenthetical structure, Wordsworth supplies clear thematic links (for example, 'virtue' in line 9 repeats the subject of line 3) in order to maintain the broad outline of a discursive, argumentative structure. The *image* of ascent in line 11 (a metaphor) becomes an *actual* physical movement in line 21. The statement of a general principle (1–16) is linked to a 'proof' from personal experience (lines 18 and onwards, beginning with 'I remember') by a smooth and prosaic transition (lines 16–18, 'Such moments . . . childhood'). The appeal of the central narrative incident is self-evident, with its sinister rural epitaph preserved 'to this hour', but the ordinary is transformed into 'visionary dreariness' (line 49), and for the rest of the extract we are concerned not only with the 'hiding places' of Wordsworth's poetic imagination but also with the inner spiritual resources of Man in general. The child is father of the man; the past penetrates and shapes the present and future; the verse paragraph shifts from present to past experience, and then returns to a present in which the past is receding:

> . . . I would approach them, but they close.
> I see by glimpses now; when age comes on,
> May scarcely see at all;

and the whole episode is described as a way of 'enshrining' (77) in deficient words the 'Substance and life' (77) of feeling. The pursuit of authentic experience takes priority over everything else, just as the design of the paragraph as a whole is determined by the process of working out the complex of thought and emotion. For Wordsworth there is 'no essential difference between the language of prose and metrical composition', for

> If it be affirmed that rhyme and metrical arrangement of themselves constitute a distinction which overturns what I have been saying on the strict affinity of metrical language with that of prose . . . I answer that the distinction of rhyme and metre is regular and uniform, and not, like that which is produced by what is usually called poetic diction, arbitrary and subject to infinite caprices upon which no calculation whatever can be made. In the one case the Reader is utterly at the mercy of the Poet respecting what imagery or diction he may choose to connect with the passion, whereas in the other the metre obeys certain laws, to which the Poet and Reader both willingly submit . . . the co-presence of something regular, something to which the mind has been accustomed when in an unexcited or a less excited state, cannot but have great efficacy in tempering and restraining the passion by an intertexture of ordinary feeling.
>
> (Preface to *Lyrical Ballads*, 1800)

The metrical pattern of the blank verse line, it seems, provides both a control of poetic excitement and a recurrent norm from which the excitement may be generated. Thus the 'prosaic' transition in lines 16–18,

> Such moments
> Are scattered everywhere, taking their date
> From our first childhood

links the analytic and defining purpose of the opening lines with the increasingly 'visionary' quality of the subsequent passage.

Wordsworth's practice in blank verse is one way, Robert Browning's is another. The unifying principle of his monologues is not only the consistent pattern of blank verse rhythms but also what may be called the psychological creation of personality through a tone of voice, as in the opening lines of 'Fra Lippo Lippi' (1855):

I am poor brother Lippo, by your leave!
You need not clap your torches to my face.
Zooks, what's to blame? you think you see a monk!
What, 'tis past midnight, and you go the rounds,
And here you catch me at an alley's end
Where sportive ladies leave their doors ajar?
The Carmine's my cloister: hunt it up,
Do – harry out, if you must show your zeal,
Whatever rat, there, haps on his wrong hole,
And nip each softling of a wee white mouse,
Weke, weke, that's crept to keep him company!
Aha, you know your betters! Then, you'll take
Your hand away that's fiddling on my throat,
And please to know me likewise. Who am I?*

Poetry and song: the lyric

Thomas Campion, 'All lookes be pale', from *Two Bookes of Aires* (1613)

*For further discussion, see Robert Langbaum, *The Poetry of Experience: The Dramatic Monologue in Modern Literary Tradition*, Random House, New York, 1957.

All lookes be pale, harts cold as stone,
For *Hally** now is dead, and gone,
   Hally in whose sight,
      Most sweet sight,
All the earth late tooke delight.
Ev'ry eye weepe with mee,
Joyes drown'd in teares must be.

If we compare Campion's lyric as a *verbal* poem with its *musical* setting
(also by Campion), three significant differences are apparent: (1) short,
monosyllabic *words* (*stone, gone, sight, be*) in the poem become long
words in terms of musical value in the musical form; (2) additional
words are lengthened by the musical time they are made to occupy:
Hally (line 3), and *sweet* (line 4); (3) the second half of line 6 is repeated
(twice), and the whole of the last line is repeated once.

These adjustments indicate the transmutation of accentual-syllabic
verse into what is, in effect, quantitative verse-song. Musical prosody is
always quantitative, which is to say that the ear perceives rhythm as in
Greek or Latin verse, as differences in duration. In addition, words such
as *stone/gone, sight/sight, mee/be* are both metrically stressed (since
they are rhymes) and musically lengthened, if we include the subsequent
musical pause as a kind of unstressed syllable.

Lyric is difficult to define, since in its most general sense it denotes one
of three broad types of poetry, the other two being *narrative* and
dramatic. A lyric may be written specifically for the singing voice
(whether accompanied by musical instruments or not), as in the
Campion example above. But since the Renaissance a vast number of
lyrics quite clearly stand as non-musical verbal poems. Lyric cannot be
defined by its subject, neither by reference to qualities such as brevity, or
subjectivity, nor by metrical characteristics: Milton's *L'Allegro* and
Il Penseroso are neither short nor particularly musical, and they are
certainly not intimately subjective. A useful definition speaks of the lyric
as being

> representational of music in its sound patterns, basing its meter and
> rhyme on the regular linear measure of the song; or, more remotely, it
> employs cadence and consonance to approximate the tonal variation
> of a chant or intonation. Thus the lyric retains structural or
> substantive evidence of its melodic origins, and it is this factor which
> serves as the categorical principle of poetic lyricism.†

Melodic origin or melodic intention is therefore the quality which unites

* *Hally* is Henry, Prince of Wales, son of King James I, who died in 1612.
† Alex Preminger, ed., *Princeton Encyclopaedia of Poetry and Poetics* (enlarged edn.),
Princeton University Press, Princeton and London, 1975, p. 461.

the *songs* of Shakespeare, Campion and Dryden with the *non-musical songs* (or verbal lyrics) of Donne, Marvell, Waller, Blake, Hopkins, Yeats and Auden.

In Milton's masque, *Comus* (1637), Sabrina's song, lines 889–900, 'means' very little, but its melodic qualities evoke a world of magic through its incantatory rhythms:

> By the rush-fringed bank,
> Where grows the Willow and the Osier dank,
> My sliding Chariot stays,
> Thick set with Agat, and the Azurn sheen
> Of Turkis blue, and Emrauld green
> That in the channel strays,
> Whilst from off the waters fleet
> Thus I set my printless feet
> Ore the Cowslips Velvet head,
> That bends not as I tread,
> Gentle swain at thy request
> I am here.

This was written for performance, to be sung, but Tennyson's *The Lotus-Eaters* (1833) was not. Tennyson concentrates on sound almost exclusively in the following passage in order to induce a drugged, trance-like state in accord with its subject ('moly' in the first line was the magical herb given to Odysseus by Hermes as protection against the sorceries of Circe; see Homer, *Odyssey*, X):

> But, propt on beds of amaranth and moly,
> How sweet (while warm airs lull us, blowing lowly)
> With half-dropt eyelids still,
> Beneath a heaven dark and holy,
> To watch the long bright river drawing slowly
> His waters from the purple hill –
> To hear the dewy echoes calling
> From cave to cave thro' the thick-twined vine –
> To watch the emerald-colour'd water falling
> Thro' many a wov'n acanthus-wreath divine!
> Only to hear and see the far-off sparkling brine,
> Only to hear were sweet, stretch'd out beneath the pine.

How can echoes be 'dewy'?, we might prosaically ask. Does 'heaven' need to be 'holy' in order to rhyme with 'slowly'? Has Tennyson subordinated sense to sound to the point of distorting meaning? Does this poem indicate the limits of musical imitation, or substitution? The effect of rhythm, alliteration, assonance and onomatopoeia creates a seductive, dream-like laziness, a melodic quality, but perhaps tries too hard. A lyric need not pretend to be music in order to evoke a melodic analogy. Blake's *Songs of Innocence* and *Songs of Experience* brilliantly adapt the apparently simple melodic origins of conventional lyric forms to intensely *felt* rhythms of emotion and suffering, as in 'Mad Song':

> The wild winds weep,
>   And the night is a-cold;
> Come hither, Sleep,
>   And my griefs infold:
> But lo! the morning peeps
>   Over the eastern steeps,
> And the rustling birds of dawn
> The earth do scorn.
>
> Lo! to the vault
>   Of paved heaven,
> With sorrow fraught
>   My notes are driven:
> They strike the ear of night,
>   Make weep the eyes of day;
> They make mad the roaring winds,
>   And with tempests play.
>
> Like a fiend in a cloud
>   With howling woe,
> After night I do croud,
>   And with night will go;
> I turn my back to the east
> From whence comforts have increas'd;
> For light doth seize my brain
>   With frantic pain.

The golden age of vocal music was during the reign of Elizabeth I, and especially the years between 1588 and 1632, the period of Thomas Campion, Ben Jonson, Shakespeare, and of the composers John Dowland, William Byrd, and Orlando Gibbons. It was not until the end of the seventeenth century that poetry became almost exclusively a matter of printed words on a page. As we have seen, oral poetry exhibits certain stylistic features related to its mode of performance, such as regular rhythmic patterns and lines, repetition, alliteration, and so on, all perhaps connected to its mnemonic needs. As Alex Preminger points out:

> from its primordial form of the song as the embodiment of an emotional reaction, the lyric has been expanded, discussed, altered, and developed through the centuries until it has become one of the

chief literary instruments which focus and evaluate the human condition.*

Whatever its subsequent transformations, the lyric nevertheless keeps us in touch with the first moment in human consciousness when man's deepest need for self-expression made itself into a song.

For further reading see: Noah Greenberg, W. H. Auden and Chester Kallman, *An Elizabethan Song Book: Lute Songs, Madrigals and Rounds*, Faber & Faber, London, 1957; Preminger's article cited above; Donald Davie, ed., *Augustan Lyrics*, Heinemann, London, 1974 (a useful Introduction is included); the lyrics of Burns (e.g. 'Afton Water', 'Green Grow the Rashes', 'A Red, Red Rose' (1786–96)); Hopkins's 'The Habit of Perfection' and 'The May Magnificat'; Yeats's 'Two Songs from a Play', 'I am of Ireland', 'Supernatural Songs', 'Under Ben Bulben'; Thom Gunn *My Sad Captains*. A good anthology will provide countless other examples. For the early period, see Kenneth Muir, ed., *Elizabethan Lyrics: A Critical Anthology*, Harrap, London, 1952. For a contemporary view, see Graham Hough's 'The Modernist Lyric', in Malcolm Bradbury and James MacFarlane, eds., *Modernism 1890–1930*, Penguin Books, Harmondsworth, 1976, pp. 312–22.

* *Op. Cit.*, p. 470.

A map of English poetry

The following is an outline map of English poetry from the fourteenth century to the modern period. Shorter poems are in quotation marks; longer poems, prose, and poetry volumes are in italics. Important critical discussions of poetry are included between brackets either under the appropriate poet, or in the last column if by another author. The date of *publication* is given, preceded by date of *composition*, where known.

Middle Ages, to 1485

Significant events: William Caxton (c.1422–92) sets up printing press at Westminster, 1476; first book printed at Oxford, c.1478; Sir Thomas Malory's *Morte D'Arthur* printed by Caxton, 1485

Geoffrey Chaucer, c.1340–1400

Romaunt of the Rose, 1532; *Book of the Duchess*, 1370, 1532; *Troilus and Criseide*, 1385, 1482; *Canterbury Tales*, begun 1386, 1478 – introduced the iambic pentameter line into English poetry

(author not known) *Sir Gawaine and the Grene Knight*, c.1375–1400, 1839
William Langland, c.1332–1400 *Vision of Piers Plowman* (B Text), c.1377, 1550
(author not known) *Everyman*, c.1485, 1510–19
Robert Henryson, c.1430–1506 *Testament of Cresseid*, 1532
William Dunbar, c.1460–c.1530 *Poems* (inc. *Dance of the Seven Deadly Sins*), 1508

Sixteenth century, 1485–1603

Significant events: Accession of Henry VII, 1485; Columbus discovers America, 1492; accession of Henry VIII, 1509; the Great Bible, 1539; Book of Common Prayer, 1549 and 1552; accession of Elizabeth I, 1558; Arthur Golding's translation of Ovid's *Metamorphoses*, 1565–7; Drake's voyage round the world, 1577–80; defeat of Spanish Armada, 1588; Shakespeare's *Venus and Adonis*, 1593; Globe Theatre opened, 1599; James I succeeds Elizabeth, 1603

John Skelton, c.1460–1529 *Collyn Cloute*, c.1523–7; *Works*, 1568

Sir Thomas Wyatt, 1503–42 Henry Howard, Earl of Surrey, 1517–47	} Tottell's *Miscellany*, 1557, included their *Songes and Sonettes*; Howard's translation of Books 2 and 4 of Virgil's *Aeneid* was the first blank verse poem in English	George Puttenham, *The Arte of English Poesie*, 1589
Sir Philip Sidney, 1554–86	*Arcadia*, 1590; *Astrophel and Stella*, 1582, 1591 (sonnet sequence) (*An Apologie for Poetrie*, 1595)	
Edmund Spenser, 1552–99	*The Shepheardes Calendar*, 1579; *The Faerie Queene*: (first three books, 1590; books one to six, 1596); *Amoretti*, 1595; *Works*, 1611–13	
Christopher Marlowe, 1564–93	*Tamburlaine*, c.1587, 1590 (in blank verse); *Hero and Leander*, 1598; *Doctor Faustus*, 1604	
William Shakespeare, 1564–1616	Chronicle histories and comedies, 1592–8; tragedies and comedies, 1601–9	
Sir Walter Raleigh, c.1552–1618 Michael Drayton, 1563–1631 Thomas Campion, 1567–1620	'The Nymph's Reply to the Shepherd', c.1612 *The Shepheardes Garland*, 1593; *Ideas Mirrour*, 1594 'Rose-cheeked Laura' (quantitative verse), 1602; (*Observations in the Art of English Poesie*, 1602; against rhyme)	Samuel Daniel, *A Defence of Ryme*, 1603 (reply to Campion)

Seventeenth century, 1603–1660

Significant events: Hakluyt's voyages published, 1599; East India Company founded, 1600; Bodleian Library, Oxford, opened, 1602; Bacon's *Advancement of Learning*, 1605; Authorised Version of the Bible, 1611; Chapman's translation of Homer's *Odyssey*, 1615; Burton's *Anatomy of Melancholy*, 1621; first folio edition of Shakespeare's plays, 1623; death of James I, accession of Charles I, 1625; theatres closed, Civil War, 1642; Charles I executed, 1649; Thomas Hobbes, *Leviathan*, 1651; end of Cromwellian Protectorate and Commonwealth, and Restoration of Charles II, 1660

Sir John Davies, 1569–1626	*Orchestra*, 1596
John Donne, 1572–1631	*Songs and Sonnets*, 1633
Ben Jonson, 1572–1637	*Works*, 1616–40; (*Timber, or Discoveries*, 1641)
Robert Herrick, 1591–1674	*Hesperides*, 1648
George Herbert, 1593–1633	*The Temple*, 1633

Seventeenth century, 1603–1660 (*cont.*)

Richard Crashaw, c.1613–49	*Steps to the Temple*, 1646	Thomas Hobbes, *Preface to a Transla-*
Henry Vaughan, 1621–95	*Silex Scintillans*, 1650	*tion of Homer*, 1675
Andrew Marvell, 1621–78	'The Garden', 'To His Coy Mistress', 1681; *Miscellaneous Poems*, 1681	
John Milton, 1608–74	'Lycidas', 1637; *Paradise Lost*, 1667 (in ten books: in twelve books, 1674); *Paradise Regained*, 1671; *Samson Agonistes*, 1671	
Abraham Cowley, 1618–67	*Poetical Blossomes*, 1633; *The Mistress*, 1647	
Edmund Waller, 1616–87	*Poems*, 1645; *Miscellanies*, 1657	
Sir John Suckling, 1609–42	*Fragmenta Aurea*, 'A Ballad upon a Wedding', 1646	
Richard Lovelace, 1618–57	*Lucasta*, 'Tom a Bedlam', 1649	

Restoration and eighteenth century, 1660–1798

Significant events: Restoration of Charles Stuart, 1660; James II ascends throne, 1685; Glorious Revolution, 1688–9; accession of Protestant William of Orange, Bill of Rights, 1689; Isaac Newton, *Principia Mathematica*, 1687; Locke, *Essay Concerning Human Understanding*, 1690; Clarendon, *History of the Rebellion*, 1702; death of Queen Anne, accession of George I, 1714; Jacobite Rebellions (1715 and 1745); George II ascends throne, 1727 (to 1760); French Revolution, 1789

Samuel Butler, 1612–80	*Hudibras* (3 parts), 1662–78	Earl of Roscommon, translation of *Ars Poetica* (Horace), 1680
John Dryden, 1631–1700	*Absalom and Achitophel* (2 parts), 1681–2; *Mac Flecknoe*, 1682; *The Hind and the Panther*, 1687; (*Essay of Dramatick Poesie*, 1668; *Preface to the Fables*, 1700: appreciation of Chaucer)	Sir William Temple, *On Poetry* (1690)
John Wilmot, 2nd Earl of Rochester, 1647–80	*Poems on Several Occasions*, 1680	Edward Bysshe, *Art of English Poetry*, 1702
Jonathan Swift, 1667–1745	'A Description of a City Shower', 1710; 'Verses on the Death of Dr. Swift', 1739	Addison and Steele, *Spectator* and *Tatler* papers, 1709–12

		Charles Gildon, *Complete Art of Poetry*, 1718
Isaac Watts, 1674–1748	*Hymns and Spiritual Songs*, 1707–9	
Edward Young, 1683–1765	*The Complaint or Night-Thoughts*, 1742–5 (*Conjectures on Original Composition*, 1759)	
Matthew Prior, 1664–1721	*Poems on Several Occasions*, 1707–20	
John Gay, 1685–1732	*The Shepherd's Week*, 1714; *Trivia, or the Art of Walking the Streets of London*, 1716; *Fables*, 1727–38	
Alexander Pope, 1688–1744	*Essay on Criticism*, 1711; *The Rape of the Lock* (first version), 1712; translations of Homer, 1713–26; *The Dunciad*, 1728, 1743; *Essay on Man*, 1733–4	
James Thomson, 1700–48	*The Seasons*, 1730	
Thomas Gray, 1716–71	'Ode on a Distant Prospect of Eton College', 1747; 'Elegy Written in a Country Churchyard', 1751; Odes, 1757	
Mark Akenside, 1721–70	*The Pleasures of the Imagination*, 1744	
William Collins, 1721–59	Odes, 1747; 'Ode to Evening', 1746	
Christopher Smart, 1722–71	*Poems on Several Occasions*, 1752	
William Cowper, 1731–1800	*Olney Hymns*, 1779; *The Task*, 1785; 'The Castaway', 1803	
James Macpherson, 1736–96	*Works of Ossian*, 1765	
George Crabbe, 1754–1832	'The Village', 1783; 'The Parish Register', 1807; *Tales*, 1812	
Samuel Johnson, 1709–84	'London', 1738; 'The Vanity of Human Wishes', 1749; (*Rasselas*, 1759; *Preface to Shakespeare*, 1765; *Lives of the Poets*, 1781)	
Oliver Goldsmith, c.1730–74	*The Deserted Village*, 1770	

Romantic period, 1798–1832

Significant events: Revolutionary period in France; storming of the Bastille, 14 July 1789; Louis XVI executed, 1793; Napoleon crowned emperor; defeated at Waterloo, 1815; Tom Paine's *The Rights of Man*, 1791–2; Edmund Burke's *Reflections on the Revolution in France*, 1790; first Reform Bill, 1832; Karl Marx and Friedrich Engels, *The Communist Manifesto*, 1848

Robert Burns, 1759–96	*Poems, Chiefly in the Scottish Dialect*, 1786; *The Scots Musical Museum* (begins collecting for this in 1787)

William Blake, 1757–1827	Poetical Sketches, 1783; Songs of Innocence and Experience, 1794; Milton and Jerusalem, 1804–20	
William Wordsworth, 1770–1850	Lyrical Ballads, 1798 (Preface added in second edition, 1800); Poems in Two Volumes, 1807; The Prelude, written 1799–1805, published 1850; Poetical Works, 1836–7	
Samuel Taylor Coleridge, 1772–1834	Lyrical Ballads, 1798 (The Rime of the Ancient Mariner); 'Kubla Khan', 1816; (Biographia Literaria, 1817)	
Robert Southey, 1774–1843	Poems, 1797–9	William Hazlitt, Lectures on the English Poets, delivered 1811, published 1818
George Gordon, 6th Baron Byron, 1788–1824	Childe Harold's Pilgrimage, Cantos I and II, 1812; III, 1816; IV, 1818; The Oriental Tales (including The Giaour, The Corsair, Lara, 1813–14); Don Juan, begun 1818, published 1819–24; The Vision of Judgement, 1822	
Percy Bysshe Shelley, 1792–1822	Prometheus Unbound, The Cenci, 'Ode to the West Wind', etc., written 1819; 'Adonais: An Elegy on the Death of John Keats', 1821; (A Defence of Poetry, 1840)	
John Keats, 1795–1821	Poems, 1817; Endymion, 1818; 'Lamia', 'Isabella', 'Eve of St. Agnes', 1820	
John Clare, 1793–1864	Poems Descriptive of Rural Life, 1820	

Victorian age, 1832–1901

Significant events: Victoria ascends throne, 1837; Darwin's Origin of Species, 1859; novels of Charles Dickens 1812–70; Marx's Das Kapital, 1867; Franco-Prussian War, 1870–1; Darwin's The Descent of Man, 1871; Education Act, 1870; George Eliot's Middlemarch, 1872; Thomas Hardy's Jude the Obscure, 1895; Boer War, 1899–1902; death of Victoria, 1901

Alfred, 1st Baron Tennyson, 1809–92	Poems Chiefly Lyrical, 1830; Poems, 1842; 'In Memoriam', 1850; Idylls of the King (first four books, 1859–89)	
Robert Browning, 1812–89	Men and Women, 1855; The Ring and the Book, 1868–9	
Matthew Arnold, 1822–88	Poems, 1853 (with Preface); 'Dover Beach', 1867; (Culture and Anarchy, 1869; The Study of Poetry, 1880)	
Elizabeth Barrett Browning, 1806–61	Sonnets from the Portuguese, 1850	
Dante Gabriel Rossetti, 1828–82	The House of Life (sonnet sequence), 1870; Ballads and Sonnets, 1881	
Christina Rossetti, 1830–94	Goblin Market and other Poems, 1862; Works, 1904	J. S. Mill, What is Poetry?, 1859; Autobiography, 1873
George Meredith, 1829–1909	Modern Love (sixteen-line sonnet sequence), 1862	
James Thomson, 1834–82	The City of Dreadful Night, 1880	
William Morris, 1834–96	The Defence of Guenevere, 1858	
Edward Fitzgerald, 1809–83	The Rubáiyát of Omar Khayyám, 1859	
Arthur Hugh Clough, 1819–61	Dipsychus, 1850; Poems, 1861	Walter Pater, Appreciations, 1889
Algernon Charles Swinburne, 1837–1909	Poems and Ballads, 1866	
Francis Thompson, 1859–1907	The Hound of Heaven, 1890	
Edward Lear, 1812–88	Book of Nonsense, 1846–63	
Lewis Carroll (Charles Lutwidge Dodgson), 1832–98	'Jabberwocky', 1871	

Twentieth century, 1890 to the present

Significant events: World War I, 1914–18; T. S. Eliot's The Waste Land, 1922; James Joyce, Ulysses, 1922; J. G. Frazer, The Golden Bough: A Study in Magic and Religion, 1890–1936; Writings of Sigmund Freud translated, 1913–38; Spanish Civil War, 1936–9; World War II, 1939–45

Oscar Wilde, 1854–1900	Poems, 1881; 'The Ballad of Reading Gaol', 1898
Ernest Dowson, 1867–1900	Verses, 1896; 'Cynara', 1896
Thomas Hardy, 1840–1928	Wessex Poems, 1898; Collected Poems, 1919, 1930
Gerard Manley Hopkins, 1844–89	Poetry edited by Robert Bridges and published in 1918
Robert Bridges, 1844–1930	Poems, 1873–1880; The Testament of Beauty, 1927–9

Twentieth century, 1890 to the present (cont.)

William Butler Yeats, 1865–1939	*The Green Helmet and Other Poems*, 1910–12; *Responsibilities*, 1914; *The Wild Swans at Coole*, 1919; *The Tower*, 1928 (includes 'Sailing to Byzantium'); *The Winding Stair*, 1933; (*A Vision*, 1937)	
James Joyce, 1882–1941	*Chamber Music*, 1907; *Pomes Penyeach*, 1927; *Collected Poems*, 1936	
David Herbert Lawrence, 1885–1930	'Piano', 1918; 'Snake', 1923; *Love Poems and Others*, 1913; *Pansies*, 1929; *Collected Poems*, 1936	
Rupert Brooke, 1887–1915	*1914 and other poems*, 1915	
Thomas Stearns Eliot, 1888–1965	*Prufrock and other Observations*, 1917; *The Waste Land*, 1922; *Ash Wednesday*, 1930; *Four Quartets*, 1943; (*The Sacred Wood*, 1920; *Selected Essays*, 1932; *The Uses of Poetry and the Uses of Criticism*, 1933)	
Alfred Edward Housman, 1859–1936	*A Shropshire Lad*, 1896; *Last Poems*, 1922	
Rudyard Kipling, 1865–1936	*Barrack-Room Ballads*, 1890; *A Choice of Kipling's Verse*, ed. T. S. Eliot, 1941	
Walter de la Mare, 1873–1956	*Poems*, 1906; *The Listeners*, 1912	
Edward Thomas, 1878–1917	'Adlestrop', 1917; *Last Poems*, 1918	
Wilfred Owen, 1893–1918	'Greater Love', 1920; 'Anthem for Doomed Youth', 1920; 'Strange Meeting', 1920; *Poems*, ed. Siegfried Sassoon, 1920	
Siegfried Sassoon, 1886–1967	*War Poems*, 1919; *Collected Poems*, 1961	
Edwin Muir, 1887–1959	*Collected Poems*, 1921–51, 1952	
Robert Graves, b.1895	*Poems 1938–1945*, 1946; (with Laura Riding, *A Survey of Modernist Poetry*, 1927)	I. A. Richards, *Practical Criticism*, 1929
Roy Campbell, 1901–57	*Poems*, 1930; *Collected Poems*, 1949–60	William Empson, *Seven Types of Ambiguity*, 1930
Cecil Day Lewis, 1904–72	volumes of collected poems, 1929–62	F. R. Leavis (ed.), *Scrutiny*, 1932–53
Wystan Hugh Auden, 1907–73	*Poems*, 1930; *On this Island*, 1937; *Another Time*, 1940; *Nones*, 1951	
Louis MacNeice, 1907–64	'Sunday Morning', 1935; *Collected Poems, 1925–49*, 1959	

Dylan Thomas, 1914–53 — *Eighteen Poems*, 1934; *The Map of Love*, 1939; *Deaths and Entrances*, 1946; *Collected Poems*, 1953

Thom Gunn, *b*.1929 — *The Sense of Movement*, 1957; *My Sad Captains*, 1961 (includes syllabic experimentation); *Touch*, 1967; *Moly*, 1971

Ted Hughes, *b*.1930 — *The Hawk in the Rain*, 1957; *Lupercal*, 1960; *Wodwo*, 1967; *Crow*, 1972

Philip Larkin, *b*.1922 — *The North Ship*, 1945 (revised, 1966); *The Less Deceived*, 1955; *The Whitsun Weddings*, 1964; *High Windows*, 1974; (ed., *Oxford Book of Twentieth-Century English Verse*, 1973)

Seamus Heaney, *b*.1939 — *Death of a Naturalist*, 1966; *Door into the Dark*, 1969; *Wintering Out*, 1972; *North*, 1975; *Field Work*, 1979

F. R. Leavis, *New Bearings in English Poetry*, 1932; *Revaluation*, 1949

Donald Davie, *Purity of Diction in English Verse*, 1952

Twentieth-century American poetry

Edwin Arlington Robinson, 1869–1935 — *Collected Poems*, 1937

Robert Frost, 1874–1963 — *Selected Poems*, 1955; *The Poetry*, 1969

Wallace Stevens, 1879–1955 — *The Man with the Blue Guitar and Other Poems*, 1937; *Collected Poems*, 1937

William Carlos Williams, 1883–1963 — *Complete Collected Poems, 1906–38*; *Collected Earlier Poems*, 1951

Ezra Pound, 1885–1972 — *Selected Poems, 1908–75*; (*ABC of Reading*, 1934)

John Crowe Ransom, 1888–1974 — *Selected Poems*, 1937

Archibald MacLeish, *b*.1892 — *Collected Poems*, 1963

e. e. cummings, 1894–1932 — *Complete Poems*, 1968

Hart Crane, 1899–1932 — *Complete Poems*, 1966; *The Bridge*, 1930

(Arthur) Yvor Winter, 1900–68 — *Collected Poems*, 1952

Robert Lowell, 1917–77 — *Selected Poems*, 1976

Sylvia Plath, 1932–63 — *Colossus*, 1960; *Ariel*, 1965; *Crossing the Water*, *Winter Trees*, 1971

Suggestions for further reading

General introductions

FUSSELL, JR., PAUL: *Poetic Meter and Poetic Form*, Random House, New York, 1965.

GROSS, HARVEY (ED.): *The Structure of Verse: Modern Essays on Prosody*, Fawcett World Library, New York, 1966.

NOWOTTNY, WINIFRED: *The Language Poets Use*, Athlone Press, London, 1962.

POUND, EZRA: *ABC of Reading*, Faber & Faber, London, 1951.

A valuable series of short books on specific aspects and genres is the Critical Idiom Series, all published by Methuen, London and New York, among which are:

BOLD, ALAN: *The Ballad* (1979).

FRASER, G. S.: *Metre, Rhyme and Free Verse* (1970).

FULLER, JOHN: *The Sonnet* (1972).

HÄUBLEIN, ERNST: *The Stanza* (1978).

JUMP, JOHN D.: *The Ode* (1974).

MARINELLI, PETER V.: *Pastoral* (1971).

Critical approaches

BOULTON, MARJORIE: *The Anatomy of Poetry*, Routledge & Kegan Paul, London, 1968.

DAVIE, DONALD: *Purity of Diction in English Verse*, Routledge & Kegan Paul, London, 1952.

EMPSON, WILLIAM: *Some Versions of Pastoral*, New Directions, Connecticut, 1960 (first published, 1935).

EMPSON, WILLIAM: *Seven Types of Ambiguity*, Chatto & Windus, London, 1953 (first published, 1930).

FRYE, NORTHROP: *Anatomy of Criticism*, Princeton University Press, Princeton, New Jersey, 1957.

LEAVIS, F. R.: *Revaluation: Tradition and Development in English Poetry*, Chatto & Windus, London, 1936.

LEECH, GEOFFREY N.: *A Linguistic Guide to English Poetry*, Longman, London, 1969.

RICHARDS, I. A.: *Practical Criticism: A Study of Literary Judgment*, Routledge & Kegan Paul, London, 1929.

RICHARDS, I. A.: *The Principles of Literary Criticism*, Routledge & Kegan Paul, London 1924.

Prosody

CHATMAN, SEYMOUR: *A Theory of Meter*, Mouton, The Hague, 1964.
MALOF, JOSEPH: *A Manual of English Meters*, Indiana University Press, Bloomington, 1970.
SAINTSBURY, GEORGE: *Historical Manual of English Prosody*, Macmillan, London, 1910.
SHAPIRO, KARL and BEUM, ROBERT: *A Prosody Handbook*, Harper & Row, New York, 1960.

General literary theory

ABRAMS, M. H.: *The Mirror and the Lamp: Romantic Theory and the Critical Tradition*, Oxford, 1953.
BATE, W. JACKSON: *The Burden of the Past and the English Poet*, Chatto & Windus, London, 1971.
BLOOM, HAROLD: *The Anxiety of Influence: A Theory of Poetry*, Oxford University Press, 1973.
GHISELIN, BREWSTER (ED.): *The Creative Process: A Symposium*, Mentor, New York, 1952.
WELLEK, RENÉ and WARREN, AUSTIN: *Theory of Literature*, Jonathan Cape, London, 1949.
WIMSATT, W. K.: *The Verbal Icon: Studies in the Meaning of Poetry*, Methuen, London, 1970 (first published, 1954).

History of English literature

BLAMIRES, HARRY: *A Short History of English Literature*, Methuen, London, 1974.
FORD, BORIS (ED.): *Pelican Guide to English Literature*, 7 vols., Penguin Books, Harmondsworth, 1954–61.
WILSON, F. P. and DOBRÉE, B.: *Oxford History of English Literature*, 14 vols., Oxford University Press, 1945.

Reference works

HARVEY, SIR PAUL: *Oxford Companion to English Literature*, fourth edition, revised by Dorothy Eagle, Oxford University Press, 1967.
PREMINGER, ALEX and others (EDS.): *Princeton Encyclopaedia of Poetry and Poetics*, Princeton University Press, 1965; enlarged edition, London, 1975.

Index

Items in this index appear under the headings of authors and subjects. Works referred to in the text are listed under their respective author, where known. For ease of reference, subjects discussed in some detail in the text are printed in capital letters.

Ovid, 49; *Elegies*, 50
Owen, Wilfred, diary fragment, 39; 'Insensibility', 42; 'Strange Meeting', 39

pararhyme, 39
PARODY, 51–2
PASTORAL, 49, 55–7
Pater, Walter, 'Mona Lisa' essay, 9
pentameter, 21
Percy, Thomas, *Reliques*, 78–9
personification, 60
Petrarchan sonnet, 42, 45
Pindar, 49
Pope, Alexander, 21–2, 30, 41; *Brutus*, 50; *The Dunciad*, 29–30, 40, 49, 50, 65, 69, 72; 'Elegy to the Memory of an Unfortunate Lady', 50; 'Eloisa to Abelard', 50; *Epistle to Dr Arbuthnot*, 62, 96–7; 'Essay on Criticism', 22–3, 26, 34, 49, 50; *Essay on Man*, 40, 50, 66, 72; *Iliad* and *Odyssey*, 49, 50; *Messiah*, 50; *Pastorals*, 50; *The Rape of the Lock*, 29, 49, 50, 97, 100; 'Windsor Forest', 49, 50, 65, 96
Pound, Ezra, *ABC of Reading*, 17; 'In a Station of the Metro', 8; on Pope, to Eliot, 97
public and private poetry, 62–8
Puttenham, George, *Arte of English Poesie*, 40
pyrrhic, 21

quantitative verse, 20, 118
quatrain, 41

Raleigh, Sir Walter, 'The Nymph's Reply to the Shepherd', 52
Ransom, John Crowe, 16
remiss, 21
reverse rhyme, 38
RHYME, 36–9
Richards, I. A., 'dummy poem', 14; 'on metaphor', 59
rime royal, 42
Rosetti, Dante Gabriel, on the sonnet, 42

rough and smooth poetry, 31–3
run-on lines, 30
Ruskin, John, on 'pathetic fallacy', 60

Sackville, Charles, 'Dorinda's sparkling wit', 53
SCANSION, 21–31
sestet, 42
Shakespeare, William, 41, 66, 119, 120; *Antony and Cleopatra*, 71; *As You Like It*, 57, 82; *Hamlet*, 60; *King Lear*, 17, 40; *Macbeth*, 17, 48; *A Midsummer Night's Dream*, 39; *The Rape of Lucrece*, 42; *Richard II*, 11; Sonnet XII, 27; Sonnet XVIII, 47–8; Sonnet LX, 85–9; *Troilus and Cressida*, 68; *Venus and Adonis*, 42
Shakespearean sonnet, 42, 44
Shelley, Percy Bysshe, 65; *Adonais*, 42, 49, 50; *The Cenci*, 50; 'Hymn to Intellectual Beauty', 42; 'A Lament', 15–16; 'Ode to the West Wind', 41, 66; *Prometheus Unbound*, 50; 'The Revolt of Islam', 42; 'To a Skylark', 63; 'The Triumph of Life', 41; 'The World's Great Age', 65
Shirley, James, 60
Sidney, Sir Philip, 21; *Arcadia*, 50; *Astrophel and Stella*, 24–5, 40, 41, 46
SIMILE, 58–9
Sir Gawayne and the Grene Knight, 40
sixain, 41
Skelton, John, 'Upon a Dead Man's Hand', 38
SOUND, 15
Soyinka, Wole, *Idanre*, 65
SPACE, 13–14
Spenser, Edmund, 21, 40, 55, 65; *Amoretti*, 45; *The Faerie Queene*, 40, 42, 50, 59, 61; *A Pastoral Aeglogue on the Death of Sir Philip Sidney*, 50; *Prothalamion*, 55–6; *The Ruines of Rome*, 50; *The*

Further titles

THE ENGLISH NOVEL
IAN MILLIGAN

This Handbook offers a study of the nature, developments and potential of one of the central features of English literature. It deals with the English novel from the historical, thematic and technical points of view, and discusses the various purposes of authors and the manner in which they achieve their effects, as well as the role of the reader. The aim is to bring to light the variety of options at the novelist's disposal and to enhance the reader's critical and interpretive skills – and pleasure.

Ian Milligan is Lecturer in English at the University of Stirling.

A DICTIONARY OF LITERARY TERMS
MARTIN GRAY

Over one thousand literary terms are dealt with in this Handbook, with definitions, explanations and examples. Entries range from general topics (comedy, epic, metre, romanticism) to more specific terms (acrostic, enjambment, malapropism, onomatopoeia) and specialist technical language (catalexis, deconstruction, *haiku*, paeon). In other words, this single, concise volume should meet the needs of anyone searching for clarification of terms found in the study of literature.

Martin Gray is Lecturer in English at the University of Stirling.

ENGLISH USAGE
COLIN G. HEY

The correct and precise use of English is one of the keys to success in examinations. 'Compared with' or 'compared to'? 'Imply' or 'infer'? 'Principal' or 'principle'? Such questions may be traditional areas of doubt in daily conversation, but examiners do not take such a lenient view. The author deals with many of these tricky problems individually, but also shows that confidence in writing correct English comes with an understanding of how the English language has evolved, and of the logic behind grammatical structure, spelling and punctuation. The Handbook concludes with some samples of English prose which demonstrate the effectiveness and appeal of good English usage.

Colin G. Hey is a former Inspector of Schools in Birmingham and Chief Inspector of English with the Sudanese Ministry of Education.

STUDYING CHAUCER
ELISABETH BREWER

The study of set books is always more interesting, rewarding and successful when the student is able to 'read around' the subject. But students faced with such a task will know the difficulties confronting them as they try to tackle work outside the prescribed texts. This Handbook is designed to help students to overcome this problem by offering guidance to the whole of Chaucer's output. An introduction to Chaucer's life and times is followed by a brief description and analysis of all his works, identifying the major issues and themes. The author also discusses contemporary literary conventions, and Chaucer's use of language.

Elisabeth Brewer is Lecturer in English at Homerton College of Education, Cambridge.

STUDYING SHAKESPEARE
MARTIN STEPHEN AND PHILIP FRANKS

Similar in aims to *Studying Chaucer*, this Handbook presents an account of Shakespeare's life and work in general, followed by a brief analysis of each of the plays by Shakespeare which might usefully be studied as background reading for a set book. Philip Franks then throws a different light on the study of Shakespeare by giving an account of his experiences of Shakespeare in performance from his perspective as a professional actor and member of the Royal Shakespeare Company.

Martin Stephen is Second Master at Sedbergh School; Philip Franks is a professional actor.

AN INTRODUCTORY GUIDE TO ENGLISH LITERATURE
MARTIN STEPHEN

This Handbook is the response to the demand for a book which could present, in a single volume, a basic core of information which can be generally regarded as essential for students of English literature. It has been specially tailored to meet the needs of students starting a course in English literature: it introduces the basic tools of the trade – genres, themes, literary terms – and offers guidance in the approach to study, essay writing, and practical criticism and appreciation. The author also gives a brief account of the history of English literature so that the study of set books can be seen in the wider landscape of the subject as a whole.

Martin Stephen is Second Master of Sedbergh School.

PREPARING FOR EXAMINATIONS IN ENGLISH LITERATURE
NEIL McEWAN

This Handbook is specifically designed for all students of English literature who are approaching those final months of revision before an examination. The purpose of the volume is to provide a sound background to the study of set books and topics, placing them within the context and perspective of their particular genres. The author also draws on his wide experience as a teacher of English both in England and abroad to give advice on approaches to study, essay writing, and examination techniques.

Neil McEwan is Lecturer in English at the University of Qatar.

AN INTRODUCTION TO LITERARY CRITICISM
RICHARD DUTTON

This is an introduction to a subject that has received increasing emphasis in the study of literature in recent years. As a means of identifying the underlying principles of the subject, the author examines the way in which successive eras and individual critics have applied different yardsticks by which to judge literary output. In this way the complexities of modern criticism are set in the perspective of its antecedents, and seen as only the most recent links in a chain of changing outlooks and methods of approach. The threads of this analysis are drawn together in the concluding chapter, which offers a blueprint for the practice of criticism.

Richard Dutton is Lecturer in English Literature at the University of Lancaster.

READING THE SCREEN
An Introduction to Film Studies
JOHN IZOD

The world of cinema and television has become the focus of more an more literary work, and film studies is a fast-growing subject in schools and universities. The intention of this Handbook is to introduce the film viewer to the range of techniques available to the film maker for the transmission of his message, and to analyse the effects achieved by these techniques. This Handbook is geared in particular to students beginning a course in film studies – but it also has a great deal to offer any member of the film-going public who wishes to have a deeper understanding of the medium.

John Izod is Lecturer in Charge of Film and Media Studies at the University of Stirling.

The first 250 titles

Series number

CHINUA ACHEBE
A Man of the People (116)
Arrow of God (92)
Things Fall Apart (96)
ELECHI AMADI
The Concubine (139)
ANONYMOUS
Beowulf (225)
JOHN ARDEN
Serjeant Musgrave's Dance (159)
AYI KWEI ARMAH
The Beautyful Ones Are Not Yet Born (154)
JANE AUSTEN
Emma (142)
Mansfield Park (216)
Northanger Abbey (1)
Persuasion (69)
Pride and Prejudice (62)
Sense and Sensibility (91)
HONORÉ DE BALZAC
Le Père Goriot (218)
SAMUEL BECKETT
Waiting for Godot (115)
SAUL BELLOW
Henderson, The Rain King (146)
ARNOLD BENNETT
Anna of the Five Towns (144)
WILLIAM BLAKE
Songs of Innocence, Songs of Experience (173)
ROBERT BOLT
A Man For All Seasons (51)
ANNE BRONTË
The Tenant of Wildfell Hall (238)
CHARLOTTE BRONTË
Jane Eyre (21)
EMILY BRONTË
Wuthering Heights (43)
ROBERT BROWNING
Men and Women (226)
JOHN BUCHAN
The Thirty-Nine Steps (89)
JOHN BUNYAN
The Pilgrim's Progress (231)
GEORGE GORDON, LORD BYRON
Selected Poems (244)
ALBERT CAMUS
L'Etranger (The Outsider) (46)
GEOFFREY CHAUCER
Prologue to the Canterbury Tales (30)
The Franklin's Tale (78)
The Knight's Tale (97)
The Merchant's Tale (193)
The Miller's Tale (192)
The Nun's Priest's Tale (16)
The Pardoner's Tale (50)
The Wife of Bath's Tale (109)
Troilus and Criseyde (198)

Series number

ANTON CHEKHOV
The Cherry Orchard (204)
SAMUEL TAYLOR COLERIDGE
Selected Poems (165)
WILKIE COLLINS
The Moonstone (217)
The Woman in White (182)
SIR ARTHUR CONAN DOYLE
The Hound of the Baskervilles (53)
WILLIAM CONGREVE
The Way of the World (207)
JOSEPH CONRAD
Heart of Darkness (152)
Lord Jim (150)
Nostromo (68)
The Secret Agent (138)
Youth and *Typhoon* (100)
BRUCE DAWE
Selected Poems (219)
DANIEL DEFOE
A Journal of the Plague Year (227)
Moll Flanders (153)
Robinson Crusoe (28)
CHARLES DICKENS
A Tale of Two Cities (70)
Bleak House (183)
David Copperfield (9)
Great Expectations (66)
Hard Times (203)
Little Dorrit (246)
Nicholas Nickleby (161)
Oliver Twist (101)
Our Mutual Friend (228)
The Pickwick Papers (110)
EMILY DICKINSON
Selected Poems (229)
JOHN DONNE
Selected Poems (199)
THEODORE DREISER
Sister Carrie (179)
GEORGE ELIOT
Adam Bede (14)
Silas Marner (98)
The Mill on the Floss (29)
T. S. ELIOT
Four Quartets (167)
Murder in the Cathedral (149)
Selected Poems (155)
The Waste Land (45)
GEORGE FARQUHAR
The Beaux Stratagem (208)
WILLIAM FAULKNER
Absalom, Absalom! (124)
As I Lay Dying (44)
Go Down, Moses (163)
The Sound and the Fury (136)
HENRY FIELDING
Joseph Andrews (105)
Tom Jones (113)

The author of this Handbook

CLIVE T. PROBYN was educated at the universities of Nottingham and Virginia. He taught for ten years at the University of Lancaster, England, from where, between 1978 and 1980, he was seconded to Nigeria as Professor of English and Dean of the Faculty of Arts and Islamic Studies at the University of Sokoto. He is now Professor of English at Monash University, Victoria, Australia.

His previous books include *The Art of Jonathan Swift* (1978) and *Jonathan Swift: The Contemporary Background* (1978). His editorial work includes British Editorship of the international news journal *The Scriblerian* and the Everyman edition of *Gulliver's Travels*. He is also the author of articles on eighteenth-century English literature, and has written three studies in the York Notes series: on Wole Soyinka's *The Road*, Chinua Achebe's *A Man of the People*, and Gabriel Okara's *The Voice*. He is author of the forthcoming *English Fiction, 1700–1789* in the Longman Literature in English series.